By gum,
life were sparse!

By the same author

A DALESMAN'S DIARY
IT'S A LONG WAY TO MUCKLE FLUGGA:

Journeys in Northern Scotland
HIGH DALE COUNTRY

By gum, life were sparse!

Memories of Northern Mill Towns

W.R. MITCHELL
Foreword by Mike Harding

WARNER BOOKS

A WARNER BOOK

First published by
Souvenir Press in 1991

This edition published by Warner in 1993

Copyright © 1991 W. R. Mitchell

The moral right of the author has been asserted

A CIP catalogue for this book
is available from the British Library

ISBN 0 7515 0018 6

Printed in England by Clays Ltd, St Ives plc

Warner
A Division of
Little, Brown and Company (UK) Limited
165 Great Dover Street
London SE1 4YA

For
Mary Hemingway
(of Dewsbury)

Some mill town sayings

Where there's muck, there's money.

Them 'at 'es nowt is nowt: if they'd been owt, they'd 'ev 'ed summat.

If thou doesn't expect owt, tha'll not often be disappointed.

Contents

List of Illustrations

Foreword

Bill Mitchell, for many years Editor of *The Dalesman*, is a lover of moorland and mill town alike. His little magazine, from its humble place of creation in Clapham at the western side of the Yorkshire Dales, grew over the years to be almost a Bible in Yorkshire. Copies travelled to the four corners of the civilised and uncivilised earth, giving exiles a lifeline back to the hills and towns of England's premier county.

But although Bill is no stranger to the striding Dales – in fact, there cannot be anyone who knows more about the region and its characters than he does – he is a child of industrial workers, one of the few who have had experience of both worlds: the dark satanic valleys of Spindledom and the wide and rolling Pennine uplands.

In this book, you will find your guide as knowledgeable and expansive about the ways and whys of King Cotton and Queen Wool as he is about Wensleydale cheese and the customs and traditions of the Dales.

Enjoy it!

Mike Harding

Acknowledgements

The author is grateful to the following for their interest and help: H. Archer, Gill Buckland (Moonraker Productions), *Burnley Express*, Allan Butterfield, J. Castle, Pat Coates, Jean Collins, Brian Crompton, Val Cutter, Ian Dewhirst (Keighley Reference Library), Mrs S.M. Dixon, Mrs Enid Edgar, Joan Edwards, Audrey Elvin, John Foster & Son, Mrs Mildred Gaukrodger, Mrs A Gordon, Stanley Graham (Ellenroad Steam Power Plant, Rochdale), A. Greenwood, Margaret Mary Haigh, *Halifax Courier*, Mike Harding, Albert Hartley, Terry Higgins, A. Hobson, Johnson & Johnson (Medical) Ltd, Muriel Kelly, Kirklees Metropolitan Council (Cultural Services), *Manchester Evening News*, Mrs E.J. Marsh, Myra Marsh, Hilda Newton, Ivan Parker, Raymond Pickles (District Librarian, Burnley), Queen Street Mill (Burnley), Onyx Ralph, Doreen Rowbottom, Roy Rowley, Enid Smith, Phil Smith (who has captured on tape for the BBC many tales of the mill towns), Audrey Stansbury, Clifford Stephenson, Eunice Thorburn, Maude Walkley Clogs (Hebden Bridge), Ethel Walton, Peter Wightman (District Librarian, Nelson), Alan Wilkinson, M.H. Wood.

The modern photographs in this book are the work of the author. A selection of old-time pictures includes a number kindly made available by the Lancashire County Library (Pendle and Burnley Districts).

Introduction

I grew up with the impression that the Pennines – a formidable north-south barrier of high, rounded hills – had been raised by the Almighty to keep Yorkshire folk and Lancashire folk apart. Whichever way I looked from Skipton, the reedy spurs of the Pennines seemed to occupy half the sky.

I knew from an early age that Yorkshire's emblem was the white rose and that somewhere beyond the high pastures, the moors and the swirling clouds, was the county of the red rose. History lessons at school acquainted me with the Wars of the Roses. Then I discovered they actually continued in the ritualised form of 'Roses' cricket matches played at Old Trafford or Headingley. 'There's nowt funny about cricket,' said a great uncle who played a few games for Yorkshire until he fell out with Lord Hawke (or was it his lordship who had fallen out with him?).

You must have heard the story of a match at Headingley when Yorkshire were put in to bat. A magnificent six was knocked. A small man jumped up and called: 'Well played, sir, well played!' His neighbour said: 'Oh, tha cums thro Yorkshire then?' 'Oh, no,' the little man replied. The very next ball put the batsman out, middle stump. Up jumped the little man again: 'Well bowled, sir, well bowled!' 'Aw, I see, tha cums thro Lancashire?' his neighbour commented. 'No, sir, I don't come from Lancashire either.' 'Then, sit thi'sen down and keep quiet,' he was commanded. 'This 'as nowt to do wi' thee!'

An enduring image for me is of a cricket match in a setting of mills – of white flannels and sun-burnished grass against sooted masonry.

The original wars, between the Houses of Lancaster and York, did not concern disputes along a quirkish county boundary, although there was a little mental abrasion at the edges. In those proud days before 1974 – before, indeed, the Boundary Commission achieved with a pen what many had failed to do with the sword – Yorkshire extended westwards to take in almost the whole of Bowland, giving Lancashire a waist like a wasp. Ancient antagonisms are recalled through short, pithy tales. 'Does thou come from Yorkshire?' 'Nay – I'm Lancashire really, but I haven't been feeling so well lately.' The story loses none of its impact if the county names are put in reverse order.

The best stories are spiced with dialect. A lugubrious comment, much heard in northern towns and reflecting a person's resignation at circumstances beyond his control, is: 'Ther's nivver nowt but what ther's summat.' In a Yorkshire district of particularly sloppy speech, a South Country visitor, while waiting in a bus queue, heard two girls talking. They appeared to be Chinese. One said: 'Whowashiwi [Who was she with]?', and the reply was: 'Sheworwiahsoo [She was with our Sue]'.

I was born into a family that had Yorkshire *and* Lancashire connections. Uncle Henry and Auntie Anne, and their family, lived at Burnley, so I could cross the county boundary without the customary feeling of dread.

I experienced, in my West Riding upbringing, the last great flourish of northern milldom. It was an age of textile towns that, separated from each other by fields – even by cornfields – single-minded and full of local character, thrived in all the blackened magnificence of great mills and warehouses, of rows and rows of terraced housing, of steam locomotives and steam engines coupled to Lancashire boilers. I was surrounded by an industrial past that had been sustained by water and steam. And there remain 'characters' in East Lancashire and West Yorkshire, but in most cases they are but pale reflections of those who once stalked the mill towns.

The celebrated down-to-earthness of these northern folk is indicated by this story of two women talking on the phone. One of them, who lived out of town, said she would call on the other when she went to the Co-op to buy a new costume and to get her husband a new topcoat. Her brother-in-law was failing (dying), and they would need the new clothing to look presentable at the funeral. When next the two women were talking, the townswoman said: 'You never came to see us on your shopping trip, did you?' Whereupon the other remarked: 'Nay, his brother went and got better, so we never bothered wi' new clothes.'

Although I am not yet in my dotage (merely in my anecdotage!), I can look back at a primitive, pre-plastic world of slopstones (stone sinks) and lino, of gas lighting and fireplaces with ovens and boilers. Life was chancy for those who worked in the mills. As an old friend recalls: 'Woe betide anyone who put his or her coat on at the end of the day's work before the buzzer had blown, especially if t'boss caught you. Then you'd had it. You were out of a job!'

Before the coming of admass (as defined by J.B. Priestley, one of the best-known Bradfordians) and the media, a modern Tower of Babel with its thousand shrieking voices, there seemed to be time to think about things. In my young days, people spoke or recited or even sang, against relative quietness. No one was in a desperate hurry. It was an age in which truly good work was appreciated, as on t'wireless. When a local man, Jack

Wilkinson, sang 'When I Marry Amelia' 'on the air', nearly everybody in Skipton stopped work to listen – and they talked about it for weeks afterwards!

Phyllis Bentley, of Halifax, wrote the script for a film called *We of the West Riding*, which captured this county pride. It was about hills of sheep that provided wool, and valleys with mills where the wool was processed. We saw a picture of a lorry with wool being driven down one of the grand canyons between the Victorian warehouses of Old Bradford. We listened to a chapel choir singing *Messiah*. And we felt like cheering. Bradford was a world wool centre then. The woolmen – Liberals to a man – gathered at the Bradford Club, where stood a bust of their hero Mr Gladstone.

It was just the same in Lancashire's industrialised belt. There was that distinguished person, the Manchester Man, who attended the Cotton Exchange. There was also muck, money – and considerable spirit, as evidenced by the jubilant songs of Gracie Fields, the lass from Lancashire. She sang of the mill girl Sally, the 'pride of our alley'. (An alley was also the space between two rows of looms in a weaving shed.) The wondrous voice is still capable of stirring in older folk the spirit of the age. Gracie is revered in Lancashire, to the extent that a holidaymaker in Capri, Gracie's home for many years, tracked her down on her private beach and told Gracie that she knew people in her home town. Gracie had not outgrown her humble mill town origins. 'Eh, lass,' she said, 'it's grand to speak to somebody from Rochdale.'

Mill town men and women do not waste words. They are witty rather than humorous. Such is their restless nature, they may find humour (which is contrived) rather boring. They are self-deprecating. Similes abound, as indicated by such remarks as 'Owd Betty's as thin as a lat.' Lettice Cooper, the Yorkshire novelist, is fascinated by the Colne Valley way of speaking. 'Where do you live?' she asked. And the reply was: 'Back anent t'Baptist

Chapel. It were slaughtering in t'wind when ah coom oot.' This, being translated, contains the information that the man's home stands opposite the Baptist Chapel, and that when he left home there was rain on the wind!

Chirpy characters are still with us. Their shrill voices or loud whisperings are to be heard in public places. A woman observed, with biblical brevity: 'Joe's gone.' Her neighbour looked sad for a few moments, then – with her mind on the coming funeral – remarked: 'It's a dear do deeing [dying] today. I suppose t'Quarp [Co-op] will have t'job.' She permitted herself the luxury of a smile and added: 'Aye – t'widow might as weal have t'divi [dividend] on 'im.' After death cometh new life. Two forthright women in the 'heavy woollen district' were heard discussing a recent birth. 'Ah sees i' t'paper, thy Sarah's getten t'precious gift of a son.' 'That's reight,' was the reply, 'but ah've telled her – "Thee wait till tha's getten twelve precious gifts, same as thi Ma."'

The South Pennine moors dominate all. Both a physical and a cultural barrier between Lancashire and Yorkshire, they have inhibited movement and made strangers of people living in towns and villages only a few miles apart. This succession of peaty hills is also a great cloud-making machine. The copious rain gives to each brook and beck a song to sing as it flows to the low country. In the heyday of textiles, such water, clear, cool and 'soft', topped up the dams and millraces of a variety of industrial enterprises, being well suited to the cloth-finishing processes.

Daniel Defoe, who wrote part of *Robinson Crusoe* while staying at the White Horse Inn, Halifax, likened the Pennine uplift – for, geologically, it is neither a 'range' nor a 'chain' – to a wall of brass. And on this occasion, Defoe was not thinking of money! One Lancashire writer, after mentioning the wild but generally mild wind that fanned his county from the west, remarked: 'It's colder in the east. That's why Yorkshire folk are so crusty!'

In the West Riding people tend to see themselves as hard-headed, unemotional, but it is not true. The outer crust conceals a soft centre! There is much talk of brass (money), as in the saying: 'A chap 'at's liberal wi' advice is generally niggardly wi' his brass.'

The Brontë wind – a wuthering wind – still blows across the 'tops'. A notice outside a Yorkshire garage read: 'Fill up for the Moors.' Was a life-or-death decision about to be made by the traveller? Would the chosen route be as arduous as crossing the Greenland Ice Cap? Would it really take a lot of petrol for the motorist to reach the other side? Hardly – yet the Pennine roads have their hazards. They spend much of the year wrapped in mist. They are soon clogged by wind-blown snow. The M62, with six lanes, crosses the 'tops' with the devil-may-care attitude of a soldier in battle. Then the 'snow dogs' howl and an inch or two are blown into fearsome drifts that bring a temporary halt to the traffic.

It's astonishing how steep and elevated are some of the Victorian and Edwardian outposts of Yorkshire and Lancashire. Or, as a friend says: 'So many places are higgledy-piggledy, built on t'slant.' 'The Industrial Revolution placed a lot of towns on the map that shouldn't really be there in terms of nature,' remarked Ian Dewhirst, Reference Librarian at Keighley, when I spoke to him in general terms about the mill towns. The textile industry, with its need for a small army of operatives, induced people from a wide area to settle in an unfriendly environment. 'Conurbations of people were never meant to live on the Pennines. Taking the industrial Pennines as a whole, hundreds of thousands of people are now residing in areas that are wet, cold, damp and unhealthy,' said Ian – as mentally stimulating as ever.

At Skipton, my home town, we are fortunate in being situated at the northern edge of an industrialised belt that extends, with few natural breaks, to south of Birmingham. From Skipton, one might travel northwards for ninety miles through delectable Dales countryside to the Scottish border, without glimpsing a mill chimney.

Your mill town man lived within easy walking range of attractive country. In spring, the chirping of the urban sparrows might be heard – I was about to make the mistake of writing 'might blend' – with the fluting of a curlew from the wilder country roundabout, including the skirts of Pendle Hill, a real landmark. Pendle overlooks a string of cotton towns and also, in the words of an ancient writer, stands 'surveying all ye wild moore lands'. Those who toiled up the slopes of Pendle from Colne, Nelson or Burnley at Eastertime would behold the long, lean ridges of Bowland and the Three Peaks – Whernside, Ingleborough, Penyghent – dove-grey in the distance.

A walk favoured by many Colne and Nelson men on Saturdays, when work had finished, was the thirteen miles to Paythorne, by the Ribble. 'Each of us might have a penny to spend at the Buck Inn. On Salmon Sunday, in November, dozens of people might be seen leaning over the bridge, looking to see if any salmon were spawning.'

If God made the Pennines, he must have been in a hurry. These hills have a half-completed appearance. At lower levels, the drystone walls give a sense of order, but higher up, walls are far apart or have been forsaken, having so many gaps it looks as though the hill has been castellated. Mostly, the terrain is rough, with cushions of *Nardus stricta* to slow down a walker's progress. The uplands are kept mown by the teeth of the horned sheep, especially the Lonk, a quite tall breed which evolved on these southern moors.

High tarns and small industrial dams, the 'eyes' of the moors, gleam against the lacklustre setting of peat and rock. Stoodley Pike, a monument that has all the visual emphasis of an exclamation mark, seems utterly remote, yet is just out of sight of the nearest town. In the old days, a forest of chimneys gave away a town's position by breathing smoke into the chilly air. At Skipton, a Mr Dewhurst built a mill with a chimney of awesome size – a chimney made of bricks and banded by iron. To a small boy, it seemed to rise halfway to heaven. I grew up within hearing of the mill buzzer that, every weekday, roared with a sound like a bull with bellyache.

When, as occasionally happened, we had a family outing by train from Skipton to Burnley, to visit relatives, Father used to tell me a little about our branch of the family. Grandfather, William John Mitchell, had escaped the rigours of an agricultural depression in Dorset by emigrating to industrialised Lancashire, here to take up work in the mills – when there was work to be had. At that time, King Cotton had about 400,000 slaves in Lancashire, and for them life was almost literally divided between work and bed. Dorset had given Grandfather his Methodism, his social conscience and a high regard for the writings of Thomas Hardy. Grandfather found a terraced house at Nelson for a wife and three children. Work was so chancy, there was a perpetual cash-flow problem.

A Baptist minister at Burnley, giving a series of sermons at about that time, referred to 'blots on our town' – drunkenness, crime and an exceptionally high infant mortality rate. These, he declared, were symptoms of deeper-rooted evils. So were poverty, undernourishment and constricted living quarters. Then, over a thousand townsfolk were living in one-roomed homes.

Trade unionism, which had been stirring within the straitjacket imposed by privilege and convention, found in Grandfather a willing worker, though he had long since left Nelson by the time strike action, by weavers, led to the town being dubbed 'Little Moscow'. When Grandfather's family were close to destitution, he organised a move from Lancashire to Yorkshire. An uncle of mine recalled an incident in Nelson when his mother's hand had been gently laid on his mouth so that he would not cry out as a rent-collector hammered on the door.

Father had a vague memory of a moonlight flit from the house – a flit brought about not by any desire to deprive the landlord of a few shillings but through sheer necessity. In short, Grandfather was broke. At dead of night, the children were urged to be silent as they were carried to the street and away to what would hopefully be a better life. They headed for Bradley, near Skipton, finding accommodation in an ultra-large terrace – Victoria Terrace – which had been built by the local mill-owner for his workers and was known as 't'Barracks'.

Bradley, in a recess of the Aire Valley, is a hillside village, between the purple-headed moor and the ings (water meadows) by the Aire. At Bradley, the Leeds and Liverpool Canal is seen on its gently curving way between Skipton and Keighley. Farmers used to wash sheep near the wooden bridge which swung aside to allow for the passage of barges. For me, the canal bridge – the catch of which closed with a triumphant clang – was a splendid plaything, if there were no adults in the vicinity. Every week or so, a local woman for whom life was an almost unbearable ordeal took her large family to the canal, intending to drown them. Happily, she always changed her mind before the final approach, and led them quietly home.

Grandfather, having 'lost' his first wife, married again. His new wife, who had been given the good old biblical name of Selina, was one of the local Gill family. She and Grandfather met at the Chapel; they were married at the Chapel; and in the twilight of their lives, they almost lived at the Chapel. A Socialist of the old type, who had once entertained the Labour politician Margaret Bonfield to tea, Grandfather was a Primitive Methodist at a time when the cause in nearby Silsden was dominated by the mill-owning family of Fletcher. (It is astonishing how many industrialists were religious. Some even met the cost of building chapels.) Grandfather wrote articles about humble (usually exploited) weavers and those who drank to excess; they 'saw the light', having an experience akin to Paul's conversion on the Damascus road. Grandfather penned accounts of visits to Haworth, interspersing details of the haunts of the Brontës with verses from favourite Brontë hymns, in the manner of the time.

Selina had many a tale to relate of her days at the mill. She had been one of about seventy local people who walked to and fro across the valley to their daily work. Grannie, as a young millworker, a shawl about her shoulders, a blouse and long dark skirt with a brat (apron) to clothe her body and clogs to keep her feet warm and dry, had also tramped to Silsden and Skipton to find work. She told me about the firm of Charles Brown & Company, who at the village of Bradley taught the hand-loom weavers the use of power looms. Such was the high feeling about the newfangled machines, at first they dared not let any handloom weaver use more than two narrow looms. The Browns rented Cross Lane Shed until 1869, when a dispute arose between landlord and tenant. To maintain production, it was necessary to build a new shed in thirteen weeks. The work was done and the new premises were given the appropriate name of Rose Shed.

Grannie told me of the days when Bradley had wool-combers. Carrying-in day (when the wool was collected) was Monday. A woolcomber called Fielding, who was very religious, would rise at midnight on Sundays to finish off his work before 'carrying in' (delivering the cloth). A neighbour, hearing him, looked at his clock and shouted: 'Fielding – Sunday hasn't gone out yet!' 'Hasn't it?' was the reply. 'Well, Ah'll sit missen down and smoke 'afore Monday cums in.'

On Ma's side, Dr Cartman, one-time curate at Bingley and a personal friend of Patrick Brontë, became the head-master of Ermysted's Grammar School at Skipton. Ma's uncle, William Henry Cartman, was the one who dis-tinguished himself at cricket, being a professional who played four matches for Yorkshire in 1891.

In my parents' day, courting was undertaken with great formality. A courting couple indicated their status by linking arms. There was no kissing in public, of course. A pleasant Sunday afternoon's walk for many was from the town centre to Waltonwrays' Cemetery! Ma was weaving at a local mill when she was married. For all I know, she was still weaving when she was 'carrying' me, though as her time drew near Grannie insisted on her having a spell at her old family home in Melton Mowbray, Leicestershire.

Most young women of Ma's age and background left school relatively early and went directly into the mill as weavers – or 'weyvers', to use the local pronunciation. The wage, though small, made a substantial contribution to family funds. Years later, when in town, Ma would pass the time of day with every other woman we met, and she was almost certain to tell me: 'I used to weave with her.' A small, careworn woman pushing a noisome infant in a pram was pointed out as a former mill girl. Yet another weaver was a posh lady, the wife of a local industrialist, who now moved in exalted circles. She had once earned six shillings a loom per week. 'I used to weave with her – and now she's Lady Muck,' said Ma, in one of her few uncharitable moments.

We still had relatives in East Lancashire, so periodically we entrained at Skipton for Burnley. In those days when many people lived, loved, reared children and died within a few miles of their birthplace, a train journey seemed a most exciting prospect. Was it safe? What strange sights awaited us in Lancashire? Nelson, Colne and Burnley proved, when viewed from the railway, to be a continuation of what we had left – an area where the lowest land was packed with mills and terraced housing that spread upwards until it petered out on the spurs of the Pennines.

When I was a child, Burnley was said to be the world's largest cotton-weaving town, a status proclaimed by a conglomeration of sooted buildings and by hundreds of mean streets. There were all the usual jokes about mills, such as this inquiry to a mill-owner: 'How many people work at your mill?' To which he replied: 'About half of 'em.' Then there is this story, dating from the days when workers were summoned by steam whistle, of the manufacturer who accosted a late arrival with the words: 'Doesn't thou know? – hooter's gone.' The worker shook his head and remarked: 'They'll pinch owt nowadays.'

In Burnley, I noticed subtle differences in the native speech. In Yorkshire, we went up t'hill and here in Lancashire it was usually up th'ill. There seemed to be a high proportion of ginger-haired folk in Burnley. Some said it was rust, and others that these were descendants of settlers from Ireland, the first of whom had arrived during the Great Hunger of the 1840s. Our Burnley friends included the Hugills, a family from Swaledale in the Yorkshire Dales, whose forebears had emigrated to Lancashire when lead-mining was in rapid decline. 'Families wi'a lot o' lads went to steel works or coal mines i' Durham, and if there were a lot o' lasses they headed for Lancashire. We met up again on chapel anniversary day at Gunnerside.'

Burnley, it seems, played a part in creating one of the wild but daft rumours that periodically swept the country during the 1914–18 war. It was reported that a train-load of Russian soldiers had been seen. These soldiers had snow on their boots! The story sent a chill of horror through a nervous nation. A train-load of soldiers had, indeed, stopped at Barracks Station in Burnley. A local porter inquired: 'Where've you come from?' One of the men grunted: 'Ross-shire.' Snow on the boots was an embellishment to the story.

Even as a boy, I was impressed by the vitality of the mill towns. The Victorians were not just content to look at the world from behind lace curtains and potted aspidistras; in this area of wool and cotton, coal and cloth, they were doers.

And you must credit the town-builders with verve and style. Many a quiet little village blossomed, in a few decades, into a busy town. In the short, sharp valleys, the arteries of communication – road, rail and canal – lay side by side and were spanned by enormous bridges of stone and iron. Those men were confident as well as proud of their achievements. When the imposing North Bridge at Halifax was opened 120 years ago, the load-testing consisted of a 33-ton boiler hauled by a team of over twenty horses. The building boom, stunning if unsightly, was sustained by a small army of quarrymen, using native gritstone. The builders ran amok, so to speak, using every available yard of ground, including the hills and hummocks. But the hills remained at the back of the mind as a special sort of scenery. Now and again, a mill-towner might lift up his eyes to the hills, whence came milk, mutton and drinking water.

The Moors were a source of physical and mental refreshment. The paths leading from Airedale across the moorland to Ilkley were well trodden during the short Easter break. Trips to unspoilt countryside by train and wagonette catered for the less energetic. A West Riding church choir, visiting Ilkley Moor, made up a song about a couple who had sloped away, bent on a spell of courtship. The lad was seen in the moorland air 'baht 'at' (without a hat). He ran the risk of catching a cold, which would lead to his death. The improvised song about Ilkla' Moor, when set to the old hymn tune 'Cranbrook', became an unofficial Yorkshire anthem.

Perhaps my love of the Moors began with Grandfather's library, which included works by Hardy and the Brontë girls. I loved to explore the Moors, this breezy no-man's-land between the white and red rose counties, where slabs of moist peat have the colour and consistency of good chocolate cake. At mid-day I would eat my sandwiches while sitting on outcropping gritstone – millstone grit! The very name has a strong appeal to anyone reared beside the southern Pennines.

Just a few vacant miles lay between the conurbations of the West Riding and Lancashire. It was invigorating to leave one of the major towns, where over 50 large mills were breathing dark smoke into the chilled moorland air, and proceed up a valley that became narrower, deeper, with mills and houses standing on ledges cut from hillsides. Suddenly, man's works were left behind. I was on the Moors. Here, the sheep were sooty. Here the crows blinked industrial grit from their eyes after flying over the towns. The few old thorn trees wheezed like asthmatic men. The occasional roadside inn looked like an embattled desert fort.

Yet within a few miles the road would be dipping into Lancashire, passing a few hill farms, the first mills, the first shops – every fourth shop a Quarp (Co-op) – and more mills, with a forest of chimneys. On breezy days the smoke from Lancashire mills, wafted eastwards by the prevailing wind, doubtless merged with the smoke of Yorkshire. In that respect, at least, the two counties were united.

In my exploration of Lancashire, I had a shock of delight when I first saw a truly large spinning mill, built of red brick, with what appeared to be acres of glass panes in the windows, a great tower holding the water tank, and an enormous chimney to slice the passing clouds. When lit up at night, such a mill was like a palace. Just before the 1914–18 war, Oldham had over three hundred mills, the largest of them with an awesome 100,000 spindles.

The vitality of the old towns was impressive. It was in the narrowing confines of these industrialised valleys, in the towns and villages snuggling against the Pennines, that the world's first major industrial revolution began. Lancashire cotton and Yorkshire wool made and sustained the late-Victorian and Edwardian trade expansion, generating much of the wealth that was poured into investment overseas. It was said that Lancashire wove enough cotton cloth before breakfast to satisfy the home demand. After that, all the cloth produced was for export.

In the West Riding, the climactic period was between 1853 and 1873. On the former date, Titus Salt established Saltaire, a model village of eight hundred homes with an enormous mill at its heart and not a single pub in sight, for Titus did not believe in 'strong drink'. At Salt's Mill, raw wool went in at one end and finished cloth was taken out at the other! And at Dalton Mill, Keighley – which, judging from its enormous scale, must have been inspired by Saltaire – stood the most powerful beam engine in the land. Wishing to photograph the engine house one day, I stood before a substantial building and pointed my camera at it. A passer-by remarked: 'That building housed only the auxiliary engine; the main engine house is behind you.' I turned, to see a building that was almost a mill in itself!

The golden period might be said to have ended at the time when Samuel Cunliffe Lister's mill reared up at Manningham, with a chimney so huge it was popularly supposed that you might drive a horse-drawn vehicle around the top, providing you could get it up the chimney in the first place. That chimney was such a landmark that many thousands of people lived within sight of it and, during the Easter break, one of the few – and unpaid – holidays in the textile year, a day on the Moors was said to have begun only when the chimney could not be seen.

A century and more go, many mill-towners strode through Eldwick on their way to Dick Hudson's, a moor-edge pub. Glancing behind occasionally, they would see the enormous chimney, standing on its industrialised ridge. A few more paces, and the walkers reached the gap in a wall that gave access to the moor. The chimney was lost to sight.

This was the supreme moment of the outing – a feeling of release from the daily round and the common task. As

J.B. Priestley wrote: 'The moors are there, miles and miles of countryside that has not changed for centuries. You have only to squeeze through the little hole in the wall, just beyond Dick Hudson's, to take your fill of them.'

1 Popular Images

Gracie Fields, a Rochdale lass, gave us a memorable image of the spirited Lancashire mill girl. Her personality – and her songs – were typical of the Lancashire spinning towns, such as Rochdale, Oldham and Bolton. Here the cotton seems to sing to itself as it is processed. In her autobiography, Gracie related that her mother was only 19 years old when she 'had me', and that the neighbours did not give her a scrap of encouragement, one of them observing, above the bawling of the infant: 'If I were thee, I'd smother yon child . . . Happen we'll get some sleep then.'

The bawling turned into a powerful, clear voice to which, periodically, she added a cheeky whistle. Gracie, under her real name Stansfield, was a music hall star. Then she became a celluloid Sally.

I first came face to face with Gracie, and with the mill town image, while sitting in the cheapest seat at the Premier cinema, Skipton. The celluloid Gracie crossed the screen, at the head of a host of defiant mill workers, and gave us her rousing song 'Sing as We Go', in a film scripted by that crusty but soft-centred native of Wooltopolis, J.B. Priestley. She did know what she was singing about, being the daughter of a Lancashire weaver and herself starting work in the mill. This involved rising from her bed at 5 a.m. and walking a mile to the mill, which she must reach at 6 a.m. if she was not to be fined.

The cinema gave us a host of popular images between the wars; it also began the process of Americanisation of the British which continues to this day. The Premier, one of three cinemas in my home town, was a barn-like building from which, on summer days when the windows of the projection room were left open, came the sound of gunfire – incessant gunfire, with every other shot a ricochet – as the bad men of the American West were subdued by such as Buck Jones and Tom Mix.

The cinema had tolerably comfortable seating for those who could afford to pay the extra coppers and sit at the back. The first few rows were plain forms. Here the children of the neighbourhood would stare open-mouthed and with back-tilted necks, at monochromatic images on the grand scale. The old *Picture Post* captured it perfectly with a feature showing the faces of a youthful audience. The caption to a picture of one tense lad was: 'Look out, mister – he's got a gun!' At the old-time cinema, one or two double seats were intended for 'courting couples'. Such a seat made it easy to hold hands, which was about as far as your 1930s suitor dared go in such a public place.

Mrs Dean, the wiry woman who owned the cinema, would not tolerate disturbances, such as when her youngest patrons, bored and restless during a 'soppy' love scene on the screen, talked to each other. She was known to switch off the cinematograph and dash down one of the aisles to remonstrate with the troublemakers – or with those who remained, others having used the cover of semi-darkness to reach the more expensive seats by simply crawling under the rows.

It was in such a setting, and under such a regime, that I came face to face with a romanticised Lancashire which was somewhat less interesting than the real-life Lancashire I knew from my visits to Barrowford and Burnley. On film, even the coal looked clean. The mill girl – romanticised as the 'lassie from Lancashire' – was in reality a poor, sad little thing. She grew up with 'bad legs' from many years of standing beside a loom, with diminished hearing from the weaving shed clatter, and with breathing difficulties from inhaling cotton fluff or irritant dust from the size used for warps – size that contained zinc chloride.

Some weavers bore scars on their arms and faces left by truant shuttles tipped with metal, which periodically left the looms at 40 feet a second. Many of the weavers who began work in the truly 'bad old days' lost a number of front teeth from 'kissing the shuttle' or from sucking the thread into the 'eye'. This operation was to be outmoded by a redesigned shuttle. Meanwhile, the affected mill girls could not even whistle, much less sing. But despite the hardships, a Lancashire mill girl, whether she was sixteen or sixty, had jaunty spirits; she needed to be optimistic so that she might face the economic problems of her little world without sobbing over them. When the day's work was over, she went back to her overcrowded home in a terrace of tedious uniformity. The standard house had a diminutive yard, which included a closet and a midden. Spring would be marked by the flowering of the dandelions and, unromantically, by the application of whitewash to the interior walls of the closet.

In the burgeoning mill towns of the nineteenth century, when King Cotton was omnipotent and a huge reservoir of cheap labour was mustered in his service, every other person you met was a newcomer – and they came from near and far, from the Dales and from the impoverished corners of Britain. What this amorphous mass of people needed was an identity, a sense of belonging – a pride in their chosen town. And this pride came about partly through the ministry of the various Churches, which cultivated the big family feeling. The pubs offered companionship and solace of a sort. Also, each little town and village had the pride that derived from a separate identity, based on the special local products – on worsted, shoddy (reclaimed fibres), fustian or cotton cloth.

A mill town image was also defined by the dialect writers, some of them poets, whose work was part of a lively working-class culture that flourished in both Lancashire and Yorkshire. Significantly, this came from the ranks; it did not filter down from a cultural elite. Like a good chapel sermon, a down-to-earth dialect poem made a simple and direct appeal to the reader or listener. Such works hold so much fine detail about life at home and work that they help us to visualise how it was with the working classes in what was then a strange new urban society.

Among the notable Lancashire poets were Edwin Waugh (1817–90) and Samuel Laycock (1826–93). What matter if their style tended to imitate that of Robbie Burns? He was writing about the Scottish Lowlands; these new writers were taking a long, hard look at industrial conditions in Northern England. The Lancashire poems tend, by their style and manner, to sentimentalise experiences which, of themselves, were grim. An example is Laycock's best-known poem 'Welcome, bonny Brid'. The 'brid' was a child born to an impoverished family; their income had been affected by the American Civil War and by the refusal of Lancashire weavers to touch American cotton.

Wilfred Pickles (a Halifax man who lived for many years in Manchester) was extremely fond of this poem and spoke it with great feeling. The baby – this 'bonny brid' – might not get many 'pobbies' (bread soaked in milk) but it would be surrounded by love:

Tha'rt welcome, little bonny brid,
but shouldn't ha' come just when tha did;
   Toimes are bad.
We're short o' pobbies for eawr Joe,
But that, of course, tha didn't know,
   Did ta, lad?

And finally:

But tho' we've childer two or three,
We'll mak' a bit o' reawm for thee,
   Bless thee, lad!
Tha'rt th'prattiest brid we have i' th'nest,
So hutch up closer to mi breast;
   Aw'm thi dad.

These urban poets wrote about conditions in the mill, sometimes trying to match by the rhythm of their lines those chattering looms which were heard on every hand.

John Trafford Clegg (1857–95) introduced 'brids' of the avian variety in his 'A Weighver's Song', which begins:

Deawn i' th'shed on a summer's day,
Th'owd sun shinin through th'white-weshed top;
Brids on th'slate are chirpin away,
An' aw whistle a tune to every cop;
Clatterin' loom an' whirlin wheel,
Flyin' shuttle an' steady reed –
This is wark to make a mon feel
There's wur [worse] jobs nor weighvin i' time o' need.

The imagery in this song of the weaving shed includes a 'straight-drawn alley', such as one found between rows of looms, and 'pickin-pegs ... Nodding their yeads [heads]'. Clegg also writes of 'warps bendin deawn like wayther-fo's [waterfalls]' and of tenters (young workers in a spinning mill) running about on their nimble feet, 'keeping in time to a steady tune/Played bi th'engine fro leet to dark'.

The West Riding, too, had its popular dialect writers, notably John Hartley (1839–1915), whose 'Wayvin' Music' begins:

Ther's music i' th'shuttle, i' th'loom, an' i' th'frame,
    Ther's melody mingled i' th'noise:
For th'active ther's praises, for th'idle ther's blame,
    If they'd hearken to th'saand of its voice.
An' when flaggin' a bit, ha refreshin' to feel
As yo pause an' look raand on the throng,
At the clank o' the tappet, the hum o' the wheel,
Sing this plain unmistakable song:
        Nick-a-ting, nock-a-ting,
        Wages keep pocketing;
    Workin' for little is better ner laiking [being idle];
        Twist an' twine, reel an' wind,
        Keep a contented mind,
    Troubles are oft of a body's own making.

Hartley, a native of Halifax, was – by frequently bursting into print – to become the most prolific and best-known of Yorkshire dialect writers. He also left us word pictures of West Riding townsfolk and accentuated their character with tales marked by dry humour.

He philosophised in verse, sometimes in a rather cumbersome fashion, as in 'Wayvin' Music', where he concludes that

Life's warp comes thro Heaven, th'weft's fun [discovered] bi us sen,
    To finish a piece we're compell'd to ha booath,
Th'warp's reight, but if th'weft should be faulty, ha then?
Noa wayver i' th'world can produce a gooid cloth . . .

And here's Ben Turner, a native of Holmfirth, having

a go at philosophy in a poem entitled 'My Birthday', in which he lays on the sentiment:

> May t'cloth as each day passes by
>   Show more perfection still;
> Ah knaw it can be if Ah try
>   An' weyve it wi' goodwill.
>
> This warp o' life is brittle stuff,
>   Though t'weft's been soundly spun;
> Ah'll try an' weyve it good enough
>   To earn th'owd words, 'Well done!'

The first strong images of milldom are based on people rather than on technical processes. We are introduced to a captive but indomitable folk. We meet them at home, at work, at play, through good times and through periods of deprivation. Despite the grim conditions, the poems are generally of a jaunty character, some of them uplifting. And they pluck at our heart strings when they deal, for instance, with an impoverished old age.

The home, be it ever so humble, was a place where people could shut out the world and be themselves. It might have little to commend it, apart from providing a roof against the rain and walls against the chilling wind, but it was a sanctuary. And everyone was welcome, as in this take-off of a terrible old music hall song:

> Call round any old time,
> Mak thissen at home,
> Put thi feet on the mantel-shelf,
> Sit by the fire and help thiself.
>
> I don't care if your pals
> Have left thi all alone:
> Rich or poor, knock on the door,
> Make thiself at home.

A coal fire kept the damp at bay. Putting a piece of coal on a fire, and feeling the warmth seeping into a cold room, was a basic human pleasure. Edwin Waugh writes in 'Come whoam to thi Childer an' me' about 'mending th'fire wi'a cob' and having 'some nice bacon-collops o' th'hob,/An' a quart o' ale-posset i' th'oon [oven]'.

I don't remember that sort of feasting, but I have made innumerable pieces of toast using a toasting-fork. The best conditions were on a frosty winter's neet, with a coal fire all aglow but not a flame to be seen. It was romantic indeed, though the heat seemed to dry up my face, and scorched the fingers that held the toaster! In 'Neet-fo [fall]', Waugh shuts the door on a wintry world. After urging that more coals be brought and the fire stirred for greater warmth, he requests:

> Sweep th'grate; an' set yon table eawt;
> Put th' tay-pot upo' th'oon;
> It's gettin' on for baggin'-time [tea-time],
> An' he'll be comin' soon . . .

Waugh delights us with his originality and keen observations. 'Th'cat pricks up her ears at th'sneck [door latch]', and 'Th' kettle's hummin' o'er wi' fun.'

The dialect writers did not dodge social issues; they dealt with hard times, such as trade depression or strikes. They gave us pen portraits of local characters, such as Owd Roddle – shaky, thin, with unkempt hair and geawly (rheumy) eye. Edwin Waugh is here dealing with problems of old age:

> Houseless, without a friend,
> The poor owd wandrin slave
> Crawled on to his journey's end,
> Wi' one of his feet i' t'grave!
> Poor owd Roddle.

T. Thompson, a modern commentator on Lancashire speech, wrote: 'We slip into dialect among friends like we slip into an old and comfortable coat when we reach home.' Thompson's stories about a Lancashire barber's shop and its varied patrons, one of which I describe on page 170, are highly amusing.

There could be no standard dialect in areas where many incomers brought their own forms of speech and dialect expressions, contributing them to the common pool. Each mill town has its distinctive accent, as, for instance, Oldham's which – according to an old friend – is 'reight in th'mouth, which flops about'. At Rochdale and Burnley, the speech is rounded – 'all vowel sounds, pushed out at mouth top'. The mill experience provided many words for use in everyday contexts. Peter Wright, in *Lancashire Dialect*, quotes a few textile sayings: 'E lives back-beams to us [behind us]'; 'Ah'm stopped fer bobbins [out of work]'; or, sadly, 'Ah've woven mi piece [I'm almost at the end of my days].'

Lancashire 'speyks', such as those collected by Ammon Wrigley, reflect the spontaneous, warm humour of the towns and include: 'If thou'd any more mouth thou'd hev no face to wash.' At Huddersfield, in Yorkshire, 'it's ossin' ta slaat [trying to rain]' and – harking back to the fireside talk – 'sam t'fahr point up un' bray that crozzil wi' it', which means that you must reach for the poker and hit a specified hard lump of coal with it! And I conversed with a Saddleworth man about local expressions, discovering that this border area – a grouping of industrialised villages – lies not 'up th'ill' but 'up broo [brow]'. A worker daily went 'tut t'mill'.

One 'finisher' at Bradbury's Mill (in Saddleworth) who left school at 12 may have been uneducated, but he was quick and intelligent. His unusual expressions are still well remembered. He worked with a tempering machine. Cloth for stretching was put on hooks (tenterhooks), then passed through a hot-air machine, which dried it. He would remark: 'The important thing, Mr George, is to keep the cloth *taunt.*' A problem with 'finishing' demanded that, in extreme difficulty, an expert be summoned from Huddersfield. The Bradbury man, who knew how to finish cloth, had the utmost contempt for that sort of person. The Huddersfield expert began to advise the old chap about the chemicals to be used, and in what quantity. His hearer would snort and say: 'That may be reet *theatrically* . . . ' When something had gone wrong, he would remark: 'It must have been a *clerical* error.'

The compilers of dialect glossaries have left us a treasury of expressive words and phrases. Many words that once lived are now dead, preserved in neat rows, like butterflies on pins. A few words have not fallen through the sieve of time; they include 'addled' (earned) and 'baht' (without – as in the well known Ilkley song mentioned earlier) and 'clamm'd' (starved). But who now uses the word 'doonkessen' (downcast)? It's a long time since I heard 'spiff' (smart), 'tew' (to work hard) and 'wire in' (to join in a repast).

Dialect, heard, is a delight; but come across a page of it, and the heart grows weary. In its purest forms, it can be understood by only a few authorities – apart from those who habitually use it. In its simplest form, it provides a flavouring, rather as vinegar flavours fish and chips. Here, to follow through this theme and the 'chip shop' association, are the words of an old music hall song which Ernie Mayne sang at the Alhambra at Bradford in 1919:

> Chips and Fish, Chips and Fish,
> Ee by gum, it's a champion dish,
> Oh what a smell when you fry 'em,
> Just buy a pennorth and try 'em,
> Put some salt and vinegar on,
> As much as ever you wish,
> You can do-do-do without a supper,
> When you get a bob's-worth of Chips and Fish.

The music hall comedians and vocalists succeeded the dialect writers in fixing images of milldom. They did so with lively words and music. For the mill workers, in their limited leisure time, the music hall was a prime form of escapism. And the music hall artiste changed his act subtly to appeal to local loyalties. West of the Pennines, the patrons responded to:

> She's a Lassie from Lancashire,
> Just a Lassie from Lancashire –
> Tho' she dresses in clogs and shawl
> She's the prettiest of them all:
> None could be fairer,
> Nor rarer than Sarah,
> My Lassie from Lancashire.

This song was waiting for the mill town crowds when they reached Blackpool in Wakes Week. Lancashire lads and lasses formed a swirling pattern on the floor of the Tower Ballroom, and sang with gusto as they danced to the strains of the theatre organ.

East of the Pennines there was an equivalent song:

> My gal's a Yorkshire gal,
> Yorkshire through and through.
> My gal's a Yorkshire gal,
> Eh, by gum, but she's champion.
> Though she's a factory lass,
> And wears no fancy clothes,
> Still she's my little Yorkshire relish,
> She's my little Yorkshire Rose.

Among the popular images was a comic element. Daft notions were perpetuated in print. The house-proud wives of Ossett not only black-leaded the fireplace; they also 'black-leeaded t'tram-lines'. At Slowit (Slaithwaite) they 'raked t'muin [moon] aht o' t'cut [canal]'. Marsden was the place 'wheer the' put t'pigs o' t'wall ta listen ta t'band'. In the mill towns, the melodic sound of brass was heard at week-ends and on special occasions:

> Here brass-banding's in the blood,
> Up i' Yorksher.
> Handed down they say sin t'Flood,
> Up i' Yorksher.
> You'll ha' often heard o' Dyke [Black Dyke],
> They're a sample o' the Tyke,
> Well, ther's lots moar summat like,
> Up i' Yorksher.

J.B. Priestley, who had grown up in the exciting atmosphere of Bradford when this self-confident town was basking in a culturally rich Edwardian twilight, presented his impression of small-time life and morality before the 1914–18 war in the play *When We Are Married*. Though Priestley turned his back on his native city as a young man, and lived elsewhere, his mind had already absorbed its flavour, including aspects of the wool trade, memories of some outrageous characters, the atmosphere of music and music hall and – a 'curious leaven' – the effect on Bradford and its district of the arrival of German–Jewish merchants with the backing of German banks. 'They were so much a part of the place when I was a boy that it never occurred to me to ask why they were there.'

I remember him telling me there was nothing spinnable or weavable that did not come from Bradford. Priestley's characters, who populated 'Bruddersford', always had honest work to do. He saw beauty in unexpected places and had Wordsworth's fascination with the transient nature of the weather – writing, for instance, about the effect of sunlight on smoky air. And he knew the West Riding people, 'with their stocky figures and broad faces, humorous or pugnacious'. He created many a chuckle. Among his most memorable mill town prose for me was his account of high tea with a religious group called the Resurrectionists – a meal for which he compiled an astonishing catalogue of food.

Priestley died in August 1984, after a long life and a short illness. He who was for many years fascinated by the theme of time, defied to an advanced age its worst ravages on the human mind and frame.

Stanley Houghton and Harold Brighouse dramatised the outlook of the forthright, clear-headed Lancashire lass in *Hindle Wakes* (1912) and *Hobson's Choice* (1916), in which plays the roles of maister and weyver, rich and poor, became stylised. By the 1930s George Formby, a Lancashire lad, was one of the nation's best-known film stars. Strumming his ukelele, he caught the spirit of Wakes Week, of the annual sojourn by the sea, with his 'A Little Stick of Blackpool rock'. Frank Randall flashed his toothless grin from screen and stage. 'D'you like these boots?' he would ask mischievously, adding: 'I'm brekkin' 'em in for me fadder.'

The Lancashire novelist and playwright Walter Greenwood, experiencing the anguish of the 1930s Depression, achieved a lasting fame with his play *Love on the Dole*. He grew up in urban poverty. Happily, his mother had an infectious love of the arts. He found consolation in an awareness of continual change, of the fact that 'nothing in this world stays put' and that 'Every spring, Mother Nature proves my point when she clothes the sootiest bush in darkest Salford with a new and brilliant suit of green.'

The artist L.S. Lowry, in many a dour but arresting study of a Lancashire millscape complete with 'matchstick' people, left us his impressions of the routine of the masses who shuffled around in the cheerless world of mills and mill town houses. Lowry had a full-time job with a property company until he retired in 1952. His best-known work was therefore accomplished in his limited leisure time, and usually by the light of an electric bulb. Recognition of him as an artist was somewhat delayed. He was once heard to lament: 'I did landscapes that nobody wanted, then portraits that nobody wanted, then mill scenes that nobody wanted.' Yet by the time of his death, in February 1976, Lowry had become the nation's most popular painter.

By great good fortune, I conversed with another remarkable mill town artist, Helen Bradley, before she achieved national fame, although – I hasten to add – fame did not destroy her innocence and charm. She was born at Lees, an industrialised village between Oldham and Saddleworth, in 1900, and was over sixty years old when she began to paint. Within a few years, her vivid evocation of an Edwardian childhood in Lancashire had won international recognition, to the extent that the *International Herald Tribune* described it as 'better than whole volumes of social history'.

She and her husband were living at Cartmel, in southern Lakeland, when I met her, anxious to have an article for the magazine *Cumbria*, that I was editing at the time. Her mill town pictures featured the same characters – it was something like 'Coronation Street' in paint. I remember in particular Miss Carter, 'who always wore pink', and who appeared in the title of her first published book, *Miss Carter Wore Pink*.

Her pictures teem with life. At the time of my visit she was working on a biblical epic, not of the Authorised Version but stories devised by Great-Aunt Jane – stories in which God lived in a shed up Springhead and a rainbow was a consequence of God rummaging in one of his drawers and finding a beautiful strip of finest silk. Jonah's whale, a kindly creature, surfaced at the lake in the municipal park!

After thirty years, almost everyone in the English-speaking world will have become aware, through the television series 'Coronation Street', of everyday life in a Lancashire street, with its pub, the Rover's Return, at one end and a corner shop at the other. 'Coronation Street' is set in the fictitious Weatherfield, a district dissected by the railway.

The appeal of this television series is something more than the social history of a street in Salford; as Roy Hattersley commented, in a thirtieth-anniversary lecture, it is about Life. But its particular Lancashire genesis is acknowledged at the start of each instalment, as the camera takes in a mill town roofscape – scores of terraces roofed with Welsh slates, and uncountable numbers of domestic brick chimneys. We come to earth in a patchwork of doors and windows and downspouts. We are in an area of tiny back yards, of middens and closets, of paving stones and stone setts. It is all very familiar except that now, many years after the series first appeared, Minnie Caldwell's ginger cat, which would curl up for a sleep in the thin Weatherfield sunlight, has been replaced by a more active cat of varied hues.

Take a broader view of Weatherfield, and you see that the railway cuts a swathe through a typical old Lancashire working-class district of terraces laid down on the grid-iron pattern. There may be only one Coronation Street, but in this fictitious town, as in real life, there are dozens of streets like it, with names that would have had a strong local appeal when they first appeared – Disraeli Row and Arkwright Street, Weaver's Row and Maudsley Street, Mafeking Street, Kitchener Street, Trafalgar Street and Crimea Street. Beyond the railway, and beside an offshoot of Albert Road, lies – astonishingly – Nightingale Terrace. Had a nightingale sung hereabouts in the pre-industrial Lancashire, when there were still open fields and woodland? Here, too, is the Red Rec, a diminutive playground, the 'lungs' of Weatherfield. The terraces stretch away in their red-brick, grey-slate monotony.

'Coronation Street' has changed with the times. Human nature changes little, if at all. There must surely have been, in every generation, a type like Elsie Tanner. She, in the midst of family calamity – with a son just out of prison and a daughter who has drifted back home after leaving her husband – sniffed her bag of groceries and remarked: 'We have to be grateful for small mercies; at least the ham's not off!' And, of course, there would be lots of puritanical, sharp-tongued women like Ena Sharples who, in the first episode of 'Coronation Street', sat in the corner shop, beheld the new owner Florrie Lindley, and asked: 'Where are you going to be buried?' Then there was Frank, the father of Ken, mending a bike in the living room, which was the fashion in those black-and-white days of the 1960s. Frank's house had a touch of class, in the Van Gogh print hanging above the fireplace.

We remember Hilda Ogden, with her hair grips, her treasured 'murial' giving a touch of alpine splendour to one wall, another wall supporting a flight of ducks – one of which has slipped, so that its beak is pointing downwards. In the old days of the saga, Annie Walker beheld the world through genteel eyes from behind the bar of the pub, representing one who was somewhat better connected, socially, than her patrons.

For industrialised Yorkshire, the television series to watch has been 'The Last of the Summer Wine', shot in and around the little town of Holmfirth, not too far from Holme Moss, on which the first of the northern BBC TV masts was set – an enormous structure resting on a large ball-bearing so that it would 'give a little' when a Pennine gale was plucking slates from the roofs of the hill farms. At times, the air above Holmfirth is a battle of the winds. Nearby Longley Farm has its own huge wind-vane, which produces a tenth of the electricity needed for their yoghurt-producing plant.

There are really two Holmfirths – that before the coming of the BBC, and the one that has evolved since. Many of us remember the old Holmfirth as a typical Pennine mill town, somewhat special in that it stood by itself and was not part of a conurbation. Nigel Hinchliffe, whose family lived here in ancient times, described it to me as being 'big enough to be interesting but small enough to be caring'. When the bottomland was used up, the hillsides were terraced to permit further building. 'Some houses seem to hang on the edge of the hill.'

The folk of Holmfirth proved to be indifferent to the film crew. 'They didn't stand around and gawp but just got on with their work.' (Filming 'The First of the Summer Wine', which demanded super-human efforts to create a pre-war era and the 1940s, was much more expensive.) Television, the end of a process of communication that began with the dialect writers, has transformed milldom. Birds now pick their way through a thicket of television aerials.

Bill Owen, who plays Compo in 'Summer Wine', has had some unusual jobs to do under the unblinking gaze of television cameras, none more so than when he was invited to perform the opening ceremony for a new toilet block at Holmfirth. (The old toilet had been demolished when the land was needed for a supermarket.) At the opening ceremony, the West Riding sense of fun was evident. Army musicians played a fanfare, civic dignitaries looked dignified, and a local grocer read an ode composed for the occasion. Then Compo stepped forward with a smile on his face and delivered a few appropriate remarks.

2   Mill Town Morning

Get up wi' thi'! Ar' ta beawn [going] to lie i' bed all day?
    From a picture postcard of a Lancashire knocker-up

Poor? Surely not. They're going to work on horseback.
    A stranger hearing 'poor' mill workers in clogs

A new day began when the knocker-up went on his rounds of the long, silent streets, where scarcely anyone had a reliable clock. Every knocker-up had his own customers, each of whom paid him a few coppers a week for his pains. His was the twilight world of hissing gas lamps and yowling cats. If the knocker-up was a pensioner, out to 'addle' a bit o' brass, he would shuffle rather than walk along the uneven pavements, beginning his task at about 4 a.m. His working day ended rather more than two hours later when, hopefully, everyone on his list had begun work at the mill.

At certain times of the year, the lamplighter might play a double role, turning off the lamps and then putting his stick to another use by awakening the mill workers. John Ackworth, in his book *Clog Shop Chronicles*, tells us about Jethro, a Lancashireman who, though employed and paid by the hands at the mill, regarded himself as representing his master's interests. If a post was unoccupied or a loom 'untented' when the engine started at six o'clock, he felt that it was a reflection on his professional ability; he was ashamed and hurt.

A West Riding knocker-up is given prominence in Eric Knight's book, *The Flying Yorkshireman*, a series of amusing fantasies featuring Sammywell Small (Sam Small for short), which was first published in America in 1941. Capper Wambley, knocker-up in the village of Polkingthorpe Brig, concluded one Monday morning, after considerable thought, that it was still Sunday: the second Sunday in a row. Social chaos ensued. Knight called his story 'Never Come Monday', and had Capper saying to himself: 'Because Ah'm net wakkening onybody, it maun be a Sunday morning. And because it's a Sunday morning, Ah maun't wakken onybody up. So no matter which way a lad looks at it, the answer comes out that it's Sunday.'

By this time, Capper was thoroughly confused. He went on his rounds, waking up his clients as usual, but telling them that as it was another Sunday they could 'goa on back to bed an' sleep i' peace'. News that the week was stuck at Sunday spread throughout the North. On succeeding days, the confusion was even greater. The Church became involved. The Prime Minister was told. Sam even telephoned the King and had a chat about it . . .

In reality, there was nothing so fantastic about the knocker-up. On his weary rounds, it helped if he did not think at all. The single implement of his trade was a pole, usually capped by a bunch of umbrella wires. One Burnley knocker-up is recalled as being 'as small and thin as th'wires on top of 'is pole'. With the pole he would tap on the front bedroom windows, awakening the sleepers and telling them the time of day, even at times the state of the weather, such as 'foggy' or 'slippy' – never 'slippery'. The knocker-up applied – in his case – piano wires to a bedroom window with the finesse of a percussionist in Mr Halle's orchestra.

Another Burnley knocker-up would bounce the wires

up and down, creating a tattoo. If he twirled them, the whirring sound would awaken the dead. A knocker-up in the Aire Valley used a long bamboo pole to which some rubber was attached. When this was drawn across the glass, it 'made an awful squeak'.

Do not presume that human alarm-clocks were always male. A photograph taken at Bradford just before the 1914–18 war shows an elderly lady in the traditional mill town garb of shawl, jumper, long black skirt and long white brat (apron) rapping with a short crooked stick on the door, not the window, of a terraced house. It is recalled that one Bradford woman set off on her rounds at 5.30, returned home for a bite and a drink at about 6.45, and then set off to the mill to do a day's work.

On a keen winter morning, the bedroom window of a working man's house had frost patterns. Paper blinds, on a roll, were fashionable at the turn of the century. The late-Victorian or Edwardian bedroom was spartan, with little more than a bed. 'If your dad was on six looms, you might have oilcloth on the floor. Most people walked on bare boards; they had shrunk a bit with time, you went up and down as you walked.' There might be a mat by the bed. Under the bed was a necessary item of pottery usually known as a 'jerry'. Children tittered when anyone mentioned it.

Grannie had a brass warming-pan. Only once did I see it in use, when she removed some glowing coals from the fire, slipped them into the pan and carefully bore it upstairs to take the chill off the sheets. The stone water-bottle kept its heat for a long time but was known to fall from the bed during the night, with a thud that shook the house.

The knocker-up, that major disturber of dreams, whose clattering wand of office urged the workers to emerge from their cocoons of well mended cotton sheets or flannel blankets, did not move until he had an acknowledgement from the bedroom. No one was pleasantly disposed at that time of the morning. From behind the window would come an assortment of gruff sounds. The trail of disturbed weavers left by the knocker-up would blink the sleep mist from their eyes before setting foot on the bedroom floor, as a first stage to getting ready for work. The knocker-up and his/her kind included in their rounds men who worked on the shift system. My godfather, a driver on the Settle–Carlisle railway, would groan if the message of the knocker-up ended with the words ' . . . and lodge'. That foretold a night spent in a billet at Carlisle.

The workers were roused. Then, as Allen Clarke observed in a Lancashire novel of 1896: 'They are spluttering about in the dark, shivering as they stick their legs into icy trousers and skirts, and wishing the factories were at the bottom of the sea.'

Edwin Waugh, in his poem 'The Factory Bell', urges young Billy to heed the sound, even though the morning is bitterly cold:

> Some folk can lie till th'clock strikes eight;
> Some folk may sleep till ten,
> Then rub their e'en an' yawn a bit,
> An' turn 'em o'er again;
> Some folk can ring a bell i' bed,
> Till th'sarvant brings some tay;
> But weet or dry, a factory lad
> Mun jump at break o' day.

In the early days, the workers were, indeed, summoned by mill bells, one of which was still being tolled in the Haworth area as recently as 1913. By then the steam buzzer had become commonplace. There was a no-nonsense sound about a buzzer.

It was not so bad in summer, when the workers moved off in daylight. You'd see the procession – the dark-suited men, the women with shawls around their shoulders and their dresses extending to within a few inches of the ground. In Edwardian times, there was a fancy for women to wear straw hats. But as the textile army began to march on a winter's morning, with the town rimed with hoarfrost and the air still, its members would be muffled against the cold. No one muffled the clogs, though; those 'caulkers', the strips of iron with which they were shod, made the area ring. To one who slept in a room at ground level, the patter of a few clogs was heard swelling to a fusillade of staccato sounds.

The barrage began with the clatter of a few conscientious workers. Then, when the main wave of sound was over there would, always, be the sound of a few latecomers, hoping that they would not be fined a penny each for their indolence. A clog with its caulkers (or carkers) seemed to make twice as much noise as you might expect. The resonance of clog against pavement was equivalent to that of a woodpecker drumming on its bit of rotten tree in spring. The sound was terrifying to a stranger, one of whom compared it with artillery.

Brighouse had mill buzzers to regulate the flow and ebb of the tide of workers, but here the morning procession was 'not too noisy, for a lot o' folk wore boots, not clogs'.

Each morning, as the eastern sky pearled with the coming of daylight, the people moved like automata, their faces grey as the dawn. The sky – and sometimes the streets – filled with acrid smoke as boiler fires that had been lazing, their valves hissing with barely suppressed energy, were raked and replenished. At Illingworth, in the West Riding, those living near the mill set off for work when they saw the steam rising. In the first decade of the century, working hours were from 6 a.m. to 6 p.m. during the week, and from 6 a.m. to 12.30 p.m. on a Saturday.

One woman who used to leave home for work at 5 a.m. recalled that her mother had risen at 4 a.m. to light the fire, to boil the kettle and prepare a substantial breakfast. Mother also 'put up my jock [food]'. Workers who lived far from the mill took their food with them, in tins and baskets. A snack meal favoured by a family at Lidget Green was home-made currant teacakes with cheese. It was tied up in a red handkerchief. Currant teacakes were known as 'Horton beef'.

How was it that clogs, a form of footwear developed in the Low Countries, became standard wear in the towns of Northern England, and especially in Lancashire? The Britannia Coconutters of Bacup, who dance every Easter Saturday, wear clogs; each manages to wear out a pair during their 65-mile journey within the borough boundaries.

Sam Hanna, of Burnley, who made pioneering films about northern craftsmen, had filmed a clogger at work and was fond of talking about this traditional form of mill town footwear, with which he had been familiar since his earliest years. Sam told me that weavers from Flanders settled in Lancashire during the sixteenth century. The immigrants had with them their all-wooden sabots. In the course of time, the sabots became adapted to the Pennine environment and to the hard, damp floors of the mills, and particularly the weaving sheds.

The clog acquired a leather top, but retained the wooden sole. The life of the sole was greatly prolonged by the addition of 'irons', several types being in use. Pit clogs (or boot clogs) corresponded with boots and came well up the ankles, being secured with natural leather laces. The toes were protected by a steel plate. Such clogs carried no decoration; they were strictly for business. Footwear of this kind might be seen in a foundry.

Clogs and shawl! For many years, they symbolised life in milldom. This shawl appears to have been a development of a smaller type of shawl used in conjunction with a poke-bonnet. When the bonnet went out of fashion, the shawl grew in size until it was capable of covering the head. In the West Riding, there were two main types of woollen shawl – a large one for winter wear, and a smaller one to be donned in summer. A shawl was usually fastened under the chin with a safety-pin. Grannie wore one at home as a protection against draughts. Shawls might be made at home or bought from the local Co-op.

Much more might be written about clogs than about shawls. Ordinary clogs for men fastened with a clasp. Women's clogs, less substantial, were decorated with brass tacks all the way round between the alderwood sole and the welt. A woman's clog had a strap across the instep. The fastener for a child's clog was a button, and there was more ornamentation. For example, the half-inch-broad toe-piece of brass was largely for decoration. Making red uppers for a pair of clogs intended for a baby was once the only time that a departure from the traditional black was permitted.

Clogs were doffed for work in the long rooms of the multi-storeyed spinning mills, for the iron-shod soles would have knocked up wood on the floors. The operatives were bare-footed. Spinners often wore their clogs and shawls when walking to and from work. But clogs were the customary wear in a weaving shed. The clog iron, lifting the wooden base clear of the wet floor by a simple one-eighth of an inch, spared the weaver long hours of standing with cold, wet feet.

Amid the clatter of looms in a weaving shed, the little extra noise caused by clogs did not really matter. The only time clogs did not clatter out of doors was when there had been a fall of snow, which built up under them until the wearer had difficulty in balancing. It was almost impossible to walk until some snow had been kicked off.

Cloggers' shops stood at almost every corner. A clogging service was provided by every Co-op society, and private enterprise flourished at innumerable little workplaces that, being warm and snug, were a welcome gathering place – a 'cal 'oile' (place for gossip) – for men who had 'nowt better to do'. Clogs were bespoke, and repairing them was usually 'while you wait'. Children in stockinged feet would sit on a form, waiting for their clogs to be mended. The modest cost of having a pair of child's clogs repaired was often a burden on family finances. A youngster anxiously waiting for the clogger's verdict scarcely dared tell Mother if that clogger said: 'Oh, there's a big crack on this clog; it won't mend.'

A clogger usually had a set of bad teeth – he had clogtacks in his mouth most of the time. Providing the irons was a blacksmith's job. I suppose it was reckoned that as he shod the horses, he might just as well shoe the mill workers! Cloggers kept the forges of Silsden, in the Aire Valley, at full stretch.

Many retail outlets in the Burnley area were supplied with the blocks of which the soles were made (usually alder wood) by Sam Smalley, a farmer living at Grindleton, in the Ribble Valley. Sam bought up all the alder he could find, then cut the blocks and delivered them to his customers on a flat cart drawn by a pony. His best customer was the Burnley Co-op. At Rochdale, one smalltime clogger lived at the end house in a terrace, where he had a small workshop with a stove, several chairs, lots of shelves, piles of blocks for clog soles and neat stacks of leather uppers.

A Brighouse girl who wore clogs because the family was poor was to recall that the clogs were purchased from the 'Quarp' at Bailiffe Bridge. 'We also took 'em there to have them ironed [fitted with caulkers]. If you had kicked your toe-caps off, t'clogger put them on as well.' A vivid recollection of hers was of the afternoon of the 'terrible thunderstorm' when, as she walked home from school, she saw water rushing down the gully by the road:

Me being me, I took my clog off and let it float down t'gully. I was hopping along, with one clog off and one clog on. T'other clog were floating. When I got to the bottom, it stopped. I caught up wi' it and tipped all water out. Then I put it back on my foot. When I got home, I had to take my clogs off. My sister, who looked

after us then, gave me a clout for getting my foot wet.
I was sent to bed without tea. I didn't get owt else to
eat till morning. But it wor worth it!

When the streets had seen the passage of the noisy bat-
talions of workers, it was the turn of the children – many
of them in clogs – to rouse the echoes on their way to
school. They would probably have had breakfast of some
sort. A mill town breakfast was a modest affair, consisting
largely of bread and dripping or bread and jam – or simply
bread, if the family was especially poor.

'I went to live in Barnoldswick in 1942. You couldn't
hear yourself speak for clogs, especially at school, where
there were tiled floors. When the headmaster got cross
because there was such a racket, he told the kids to walk
on their toes. It was hard work and it made 'em look bow-
legged.' In the school yard, well drilled schoolchildren
would form up in lines to have their hands, hair, nails –
and clogs – checked for cleanliness. If the clogs were new,
they would still be dull. The dullness would be noted,
but no action was taken for a week or two, so that the
owner had a chance to polish them until they shone.
'Blacking' was used to this end. A diligent polisher soon
had his clogs shining like Japanese lacquer. At Barnoldswick, 'we used to love to shine our clogs and I tried to
get a better shine than anybody else.'

The mill town morning reverberated as children, under
the eyes of their teachers, *marched* into their classrooms,
here to absorb yet more about the Three Rs – Reading,
Riting and Rithmetic (four Rs, if you included Religious
Instruction) – which were the base on which the edu-
cational system rested.

The school buildings included premises formerly used
by the various religious denominations, and new council
schools, the stonework of which looked bone-white for a
while amid the urban blackness. The primary teachers
were mainly spinsters; it was recognised that if a teacher

married, she would give up work. The women who did not marry, and who attended school wearing high-necked blouses and long dark skirts, were dedicated and good at their job. They were strict disciplinarians. 'If we didn't pay attention, we were caned or had to stay in school to learn sums. Or perhaps we'd be told to write a hundred lines.' Showing respect for the teacher was not restricted to school hours. 'I remember one headmistress was so stern and so strict that if I met her in the street I instinctively held my shoulders back, swallowed whatever sweets I was eating, and said, politely: "Good morning, miss."'

Schoolchildren were expected to be clean and tidy. A boy from a better-off family, early this century, wore a gansey (jersey), knickerbocker trousers that buttoned below the knee, and boots with buttons. 'I remember wearing an Eton collar, made from celluloid which could be washed or sponged to keep it clean. I had a starched linen collar on Sunday.' Inevitably, in a society of varying degrees of affluence, there were a few children who arrived at school in bare feet, or with 'pants behind out'.

Years ago, some attended school for only part of the day, the other part being spent at the mill. Such half-time working was permitted by law until 1922. 'There was no shame about being a half-timer,' said a Brighouse man. 'It was just a fact of life.' Two mill jobs given to half-timers were joining broken threads between thumb and finger (they were dubbed 'little pieceners'), and taking the full bobbins from the mules or spinning frames – these young workers were known as 'doffers'.

One girl aged twelve, who began work at Rushforth's in Bingley in 1910, walked to the mill from Gilstead in the morning, and in the afternoon she walked to school at Eldwick. She started work at 6 a.m. In the following week, the first half of the day was spent at school and she attended the mill in the afternoon. She decribed work at the mill: 'It was very cold, as there was no heating.

Everything ran by steam. The overlookers were strict. I was so small I stood on a box to put the "rovings" in at the back of the spinning machine. I got the princely sum of 2s 6d a week at first, with a few shillings' rise as time went on . . . We got three days' holiday at Bingley-tide [Wakes Week] and two days at Christmas.'

A worsted mill at Shipley was the spot where another twelve-year-old began work as a half-timer on 23 February 1911. His first job, as 'bobbin ligger', consisted of carrying a kidney-shaped tub suspended from one shoulder by a leather strap. The tub held empty bobbins for the spinning frame. This boy was so small he could scarcely reach the pegs on the rail where the bobbins had to be placed. He became a doffer. The head doffer would shout 'Doff 'ere!', and the young lads would rush to remove the full bobbins. The head doffer re-started the machine as soon as possible.

Meanwhile, the streets of the mill town were rarely still, as the morning wore on and women who were not at the mill waged their everlasting war against grime. 'It was spit and polish all the time,' said a man at Oswaldtwistle. Each week the flagstone outside the front door was scrubbed down and a rubbing (or donkey) stone, available in white, cream and buff, was applied to colour it. A stranger to a northern mill town would experience the ever-fascinating sight of a woman cleaning the outside of the bedroom windows by leaning out backwards. She would push up the lower frame so that she could sit on the window ledge, with legs dangling inside the bedroom. She would then lower the frame and apply the wash leather vigorously to the glass. The window sills were scrubbed. A rubbing stone was applied to bring a touch of brightness to the façade of the house.

On a dry and breezy Monday morning, the back streets were transformed by washing that had been strung from clothes lines to dry. So dense was the assembly of sheets and blankets that it was impossible to see even halfway down the street. The sheets smacked themselves with a sound like a whipcrack or billowed out regally, like the sails of a clipper rounding the Cape of Good Hope. The impressive collection, ranging from blankets to dusters, and taking in top- and underclothes, pillow-cases, curtains and clusters of handkerchiefs, was supported by innumerable wooden props, the washing being held in place by wooden pegs bought at the door from the nomadic gipsy women.

An early start was vital for the operation to be completed before nightfall. Water was boiled in a three-legged boiler made of zinc. The housewife got up early, filled the boiler, fixed on the gas pipe, ignited the gas and then got on with other tasks while the water was warming up.

A Brighouse woman recalled how she watched her mum put the 'whites' in the side boiler, which was an integral part of the fireplace; she 'possed' them down – pushed them and stirred them around – with 'a little copper posser', and she then took them out to put them through the traditional routine of rinsing, blueing, rinsing again and starching. Then out came the wash-tub, within which clothes were stirred by a posser or, earlier, by a dolly – a three-legged device with a vertical shaft and a handle for twirling. 'You sweated all day with the dolly – up and down and round; lift and turn, lift and turn – and you added a bit of dolly blue to the water to whiten the clothes.'

If the children were about home, for the holidays or before or after school, they were recruited to help – for instance, by turning the handle of the mangle – a device consisting of two rollers, through which the washing was fed. It was important to mangle while the clothes were a little damp, after they had been taken in from the line. A first-rate mangler did the work so well that 'them clothes won't need a lot of ironing'. The mangling operation was sometimes performed to a tune, either 'Onward Christian

Soldiers', which had been composed in the West Riding, or 'John Brown's Body'. 'The mangle had wooden rollers; you had to turn the handle. If you turned it too quick, it didn't mangle properly so you had to do it again. As we got a little better-off, we bought a table mangle. When it wasn't being used on wash day, it had a top on it like a table.'

The ritual of separating clothes and dirt was an utterly wearying routine: possing, scrubbing, boiling, blueing and starching, mangling, dampening, folding and ironing – hours of back-breaking work which left Mother limp but, if all had gone well, relatively happy. And as if their own large family washes were not enough, some women were driven by a need for extra cash to wash the clothes of richer families. In the depressing 1920s, a Cleckheaton woman spent whole Mondays washing and ironing for a family with five sons. She was paid 2s and a fat-pot (a 2lb jar full of dripping from the week-end joint). At that difficult period, when many were jobless and hungry, the dripping was more welcome than the money.

The villain on washday was the coalman, with his horse and cart. 'If he decided to come up the back street, you'd soon have twenty or thirty housewives threatening him . . . It was certain death for a coalman or dustman to go up a back street on washing day.' Usually the first of the street traders on a mill town morning was the milkman, with his horse and float. Milk still warm from the cow, plus a few cow hairs, was ladled out from a 'kit' (a large can) in the cart, using a long-handled 'dipper'.

Rag and bone men were common. It was a business that did not need much capital. Children collected empty jam jars and sold them to these worthies for a few coppers. At Burnley, Rag Jack stored his rags on a cart drawn by a donkey that always looked 'starved to death'. Rag Jack would perch on the cart, and as they went round the back streets he called, musically: 'Any rags or bones today?' Mothers with naughty children would say:

'Behave yourselves. Rag Jack's coming! He's shouting: "Any boys or girls today?"'

The muffin man announced his presence with a bell. On his head was an enormous basket, lined with spotless linen. Another clean piece of cloth covered his oatcakes, his crumpets and muffins. Another street trader made a living out of clothes props, nothing else. As he passed a door, he kicked it with his clog. Clonk! Simultaneously, he shouted: 'Props!'

The morning drew to a close with the dinnertime smells, though on washday the mid-day meal was usually cold meat, the left-overs from Sunday, with fried-up potatoes and cabbage.

No one rushed home for dinner on a Monday.

3   Thousands of Mills

*What we are looking at here [a large steam engine] is the answer
to an alchemist's dream. You take earth, fire, water – and make
gold out of it.*
                    Stanley Graham, referring to the textile industry

*At Huddersfield, in the 1970s, they wove some cloth that was
retailing at Harrods at £900 a suit length. It had some gold
threads running through it. G-o-l-d! Every night, they kept
what they hadn't used in the safe.*
                            A former mill director, Saddleworth

Joe Bates, of Brierfield, climbed Pendle Hill at least fifty
times a year. His special joy was sitting on the rim of the
hill during the Wakes Week, when the workers were on
holiday, the mills were closed and the smog vanished
from the Calder Valley. Joe counted 220 mill chimneys on
the stretch from Colne to Padiham. Such was the impact
of textiles on one part of East Lancashire.

A man who undertook repairs to the fabric of mills in
the 1950s told me that one sunny day he carried his jock
(snack meal) to the roof of a high mill in Burnley. As he
ate his sandwiches and drained his thermos flask, he
counted chimneys. His best figure was ninety-seven –
'and that didn't include Rose Grove'. Geoffrey Moorhouse, the travel writer, was born and reared at Ains-

48

worth. It was then a distinctive village looking out over unspoiled countryside. He commented: 'During Wakes Week, when the mill boilers were put out and the smoke cleared, you could count 137 mill chimneys.'

Muck and money! The money was discriminating; the muck affected everyone. Even Skipton, 'gateway to the Yorkshire Dales', had its smog, for the town lies at the meeting place of valleys and has moorland on most sides. When the air was slack, it was tainted with smoke from the mills, which blended with domestic smoke and that force-fed into the atmosphere by steam locomotives at a busy station and goods yard. The soot acted as a fungicide. No mill town roses suffered from black spot.

To the Victorians, the mills were not 'satanic'. They regarded what they had built as a marvellous example of man's ingenuity and enterprise. If the chimneys were smoking, then the machines were chattering and cash was pouring in. The Cravens of Keighley, who during the 1870s built the far-spreading Dalton Mill for worsted manufacture, made a special feature of the chimney: it had a viewing platform! John Henry Craven lived at a house beside the mill where the view was limited. So he had a staircase incorporated in the chimney, and took his guests up the steps to a lookout position that was not quite at the chimney top. It offered a splendid view of the town and its surrounding moors.

At Keighley, the Industrial Revolution began in about 1780, but the place kept its market town flavour until well into the nineteenth century before making its mark with worsteds, machinery – and mangles! Ian Dewhirst says: 'Apparently, Keighley and Accrington made the bulk of the country's mangles.'

There is a strong historic link between Keighley and Langcliffe, by the upper Ribble, which lies not far from my home. Almost every morning, I walk 'round the locks' and have a view of Langcliffe High Mill, one of the very few remaining Arkwright mills. The High Mill was con-

structed in 1783 by the Clayton brothers and a Mr Walsh-
man, who had established at Keighley, in 1780, what is
said to have been the first cotton-spinning mill in Yorkshire. The Claytons were personal friends of Richard Arkwright, the Preston barber who patented a system of spinning by rollers, so that a cotton thread strong enough to
make a warp was produced. Arkwright also took out patents for improvements in carding, roving and other spinning machinery. When the hand-workers heard of these
inventions, they threatened Arkwright, and he fled the
county.

Arkwright advised on the Langcliffe project. He is said
to have supervised the installation of the machines. The
Langcliffe workers were given tuition at the Arkwright
factory at Cromford, in Derbyshire. Langcliffe High Mill,
with its river weir and long dam, is now owned by paper-
makers. On my morning walk, in winter, I observe rows
of lighted windows in the gloom and, crossing the river
by footbridge, in the company of heron and dipper, grey
wagtail and kingfisher, pass mill cottages, the most
imposing of which were built for the overlookers.

The weir has a 'salmon ladder', and the old mill dam
holds some clucking, head-jerking waterhens as well as
assorted ducks. And the Arkwright mill, though somewhat extended, is seen rising in its eighteenth-century
elegance, for the proportions are just right. It is usually
quiet here, yet sixty years ago, when the Christie family
employed 250 workers, wild birds would flee as a buzzer
roused echoes in the dale at 7.40 a.m., with another blast
three minutes later. An old lady who was one of the mill-
girls of the 1930s recalled that at the sound of the first
buzzer she usually dressed and lay down on her bed,
awaiting the second buzzer. Father would shout up the
stairs: 'Are you coming?' 'Yes,' she would reply. 'And
so's Christmas!' he would yell, knowing that a late-comer
was directed to the 'penny hole' in the mill yard, where

his or her name was recorded and a penny docked from the week's wages.

Many of the West Riding mills began with the processing of cotton. This was in part because Lancashire had become industrialised, through the invention of ingenious machines, a little earlier than Yorkshire, and so had tended to monopolise the wool market. None the less, Yorkshire had a long and proud history connected with wool. Yorkshire mills were usually dedicated to the manufacture of worsteds, a cloth produced from raw wool from which the short fibres have been removed by combing. (The name is said to be derived from Worstead, a village in Norfolk, where the woollen industry was once important.)

The mill mania that filled the South Pennine valleys with factories might be said to have begun in the 1840s and to have peaked about 1860, though it was simply an acceleration of happenings in the eighteenth century. Those little mills with short, square chimneys made of dressed gritstone were the forerunners of industrial complexes, with buildings rising to a hundred feet and chimneys twice as high. They were an early stage in the development of palatial spinning mills made of Accrington brick, which gleamed in the thin northern sunlight.

Dozens of ancillary firms, including the makers and repairers of machines, formed part of the so-called Industrial Revolution. There grew up in adjacent areas – Lancashire and the West Riding – the biggest industrial complex the world had ever seen, a complex which drew in raw materials, wool, cotton and hair, from the Antipodes to the Americas, and processed them for sale as cloth throughout the civilised world.

Traces of industrialisation are found on what are now quiet stretches of the uplands, as well as in the populous valleys. Those who take the moorland road from Keighley to Hebden Bridge see my personal favourite, the most attractive Pecket Mill Shed, standing at an elevation of

800 feet. This early-nineteenth-century mill, its form reflected in a small mill dam, has for long been devoted to corduroys. Like many another early shed, it was erected 'on spec', offering space and power for hire to those who wished to instal looms. Its steam engine was powered by coal brought in horse-drawn carts up the long hill from Hebden Bridge. The workforce, which peaked at about 250, was drawn from the farms and cottages spread along the moor-edge.

At Pecket Mill Shed, pride is evident in the state of the building, in the well-cared-for iron sign giving the shed's name and date of establishment, and in the retention of many of the old furnishings. After parking my car in the mill yard, I climbed a flight of steps to a red-painted door leading to a passage between the office and the waiting room. This most peaceful place, far from the clatter of the large weaving shed, held samples of the firm's products and textile magazines for the edification of visitors. Much has changed behind the stylish façade of Pecket Mill, but in the waiting room at least I could imagine life as it was over a century ago.

At Queen Street Mill, Burnley, visitors see a large urban mill that was constructed towards the end of the last century, by which time much experience had been gleaned on how to put a mill together. Today, Queen Street is virtually the last of the weaving establishments where Lancashire looms are powered by steam from Lancashire boilers. Its genesis is similar to Pecket Mill Shed's. It was built on spec in 1894, providing room and power. Queen Street began as a co-operative, and eventually it held over a thousand busy looms.

Saltaire and Manningham in the Aire Valley of Yorkshire, mentioned in the Introduction, have gargantuan mills. It is related that Titus Salt's vision of 'a palace of industry' came to him as he stood on the Knoll, near Shipley, and beheld the Aire Valley. Noticing the railway and the canal in close proximity and in attractive surroundings, he determined to build here Europe's most wonderful mill, adding to the scheme a complete village, to be called Saltaire, where his workers would be adequately housed.

At Manningham Mills, Samuel Cunliffe Lister built to a ground plan prepared by Andrews & Pepper of Bradford. The project included eleven acres of flooring. Vast quantities of dressed stone were taken from local quarries. Stylish lodges, designed to hold various departments, were situated along the frontage. It is recorded that some 3000hp was needed to drive the machinery.

Such massive structures, in Yorkshire and Lancashire, draw the eyes of the visitor skywards – up, up, up, in dizzying verticals – until he or she feels a crick at the back of the neck. It amazes strangers to stand close to such an awesome creation as Manningham. I parked my car in the shadow of the 249-foot-high chimney and marvelled at the Victorian verve and confidence that led to its construction. The base of the chimney rests on a bed of concrete four feet thick and forty feet square. Its total weight has been estimated at 8,000 tons, and it cost about £10,000 to build. The founder of Manningham Mills was so proud of his chimney that on its completion he went to the top, sipped some wine and christened the ornate structure 'Lister's Pride'.

Only slightly less impressive – if size be the criterion – is the chimney at Black Dyke Mills in the hilltop setting of Queensbury, near Bradford. And among the biggest of the West Riding mills is Bowling Mill, at Dean Clough, Halifax, where in recent times a group of young people raised money for charity by abseiling 90 feet down the side of this man-made cliff. The historical process that brought all this into being was for many years a domestic system, but by 1800 – according to the historian William White – there were already, from Leeds to the Lancashire border, almost six thousand master clothiers. They employed their families, and also more than 30,000 other people.

Handloom weaving allied to farming, though more often associated with the West Riding, was to be found on each side of the Pennines, as at Mellor, in Lancashire, where in 1770 – as recorded by William Ratcliffe – 'the land was occupied by between fifty and sixty farmers . . . and out of these there were only six or seven who raised their rents directly from the produce of the farms; all the rest got their rents partly in some branch of trade, such as spinning and weaving woollen, linen or cotton.'

From 1788 until the century's end was 'the golden age of this trade'. Increased yarn supplies enabled higher wages to be earned, and whole families concentrated on handloom weaving. But by 1806, with the development of the factory system, the wages of the handloom weavers were declining. A census at Burnley about the 1820s revealed an average weekly wage of 1s 8½d. A man had to try to live on less than three pence per day. For a time, the domestic and mill systems overlapped. Early mills were powered by water from becks and rivers which, later, would provide the water to meet the thirst of the steam engines and boilers.

It is worthwhile, briefly, to consider the brilliant inventions of the age. John Kay's invention of the fly-shuttle in 1733 benefited the handloom weaver by permitting the shuttle to be 'thrown'. His son, Robert, added the 'drop box', which enabled a weaver to work with shuttles containing different-coloured threads. There was no further need to substitute one shuttle for another directly by hand.

These inventions increased productivity, which in turn led to a grave shortage of yarn – if the expansion in trade was to be maintained – and so an increase in spinning capability was called for. The answer came in 1764 when

James Hargreaves, a weaver living at Stanhill near Blackburn, produced (in secret) the spinning-jenny. Secrecy was important, to avoid the wrath of those who would be made redundant by such an invention. Hargreaves lost a batch of machines at the hands of a mob of Blackburn men.

As well as introducing his system of spinning by rollers, Richard Arkwright took out patents on other devices. The need for a fine yarn, to be produced on a large scale, was met by the 'mule' invented by Samuel Crompton of Bolton in the 1770s. It was a hybrid: a combination of the principles of the spinning-jenny of Hargreaves and the rollers of Arkwright. Finally, in the 1780s, the Revd Edmund Cartwright allowed the industry to absorb the greater amount of yarn by inventing a loom noted for its rapidity of weaving – the power loom, indeed, which had its first commercial success at mills in Glasgow.

Industrial and social changes produced a violent undercurrent, as proud artisans faced redundancy. There was probably an echo of this in the custom, long continued, of firing off a mill gun at 9 or 10 o'clock in the morning to let the owner know that all was well. At Dewsbury in Yorkshire, the gun was 'a sort of blunderbuss'. It was still in action as recently as the 1920s.

There is beauty of form in the multi-storeyed spinning mill; the large number of windows gives it an airy appearance that belies its bulk. It has been calculated that one of the larger spinning mills absorbed about four million bricks, as well as two acres of glass for the windows and over two thousand tons of steel and iron, the iron beams reducing the fire risk where cotton was being worked. The large tower held a capacious water tank, linked to the sprinkler system.

A mill fire was an awesome spectacle. In the big mills and warehouses, floors became impregnated with oil and grease; the fire risk was particularly high in the days when gas was used for illumination, although successive inquiries into fires led to a suspicion that many were caused by employees who had broken the rules by smoking in the toilet areas. A six-storey spinning mill in Lancashire was so well devised for the spread of fire that it might burn out in an hour. The artist Helen Bradley, brought up near Oldham – the setting for palatial mills – once painted a fire and recalled that it began at the top of the building. A horrified crowd had watched the red glow moving downwards from floor to floor.

The mill chimneys, built from the inside, with many Yorkshire examples being constructed of well dressed stone, reached the ultimate in design and height with the use of red brick. This was the sort that in recent times was to be felled by such as Blaster Bates and Fred Dibnah, steeplejacks extraordinary. I remember Blaster relating that a good demolition man was one who had all his fingers and did not talk in a high-pitched voice. Fred's mighty deeds were featured on television as he toppled chimneys to order. Having brought a chimney crashing down before the eye of the television camera, he would stand beside an enormous heap of red bricks from which dust was swirling and say, with a toothy grin: 'Did you like that?'

Pecket Mill Shed's original stone chimney was extended in brick, but was then reduced to its original height again, now serving merely – in this electrical age – as the mill's incinerator!

The mill country of south-west Yorkshire was once a world of its own – a hilly world with the frontier towns at Leeds, Bradford, Huddersfield and Halifax. The range of products was impressive, taking in fine worsted and corduroy, velvet and blazer cloth, green baize and cashmere, tweed and knitting wools. Then into the area came mohair. And dazzling creations became possible when man-made fibres extended the range.

Lancashire's mill country lay to the south of the county

and then formed a crescent extending into the north-east, with isolated textile towns like Preston. The 'border' town of Barnoldswick found pride in weaving the blue material used for making the present Queen's 'going away' suit following her marriage. A local lady told me: 'I have an inch of that cloth somewhere. We didn't know about the Royal connections until after it was dispatched. Everyone who had helped to weave it was given a sample piece.'

Rochdale, thought of as a great centre for spinning cotton, also achieved fame for blending wool and cotton as flannel – grey flannel, pyjama flannels and shirting (white, with fine black lines), though this product was going out of fashion as early as the 1920s. The several high-lying villages known collectively as Saddleworth had flannel mills, too. The owner of one of them would receive, each Monday morning, representatives of the wool merchants who supplied the raw material. They would assemble in his waiting room, and in due course he would summon them in turn. At one time when trade was bad, the owner walked into the waiting room and said: 'If anyone here isn't wearing a flannel shirt, he needn't wait.' Saddleworth became famous for tartans; indeed, in the 1950s, Bradbury's Mill had become the largest manufacturer of tartans in Britain.

The soot-black chimneys that spiked the Pennine skies were not constructed for show, nor indeed to carry smoke clear of residential areas. The height was mainly to create a draught for the boiler. The degree of local pollution was staggering. In the bad old days seven tons of soot a year fell on each square mile of Bolton. At Yeadon, it was said of a man who was fond of his old clay pipe: 'He puffs worse than Billy Murg's chimney.' Moorland mist thickened into fog, and fog merged with smoke in the valleys to become smog. The mill chimneys were not the only pollutants, though. A Saddleworth man recalls the railway locomotives which filled the sky with smoke as they toiled upbank. 'Anything that was allergic to sulphur could not grow. When they electrified the route via Wood-head Tunnel, species of plants that had not been seen for a hundred years began to be seen again.'

As the years went by it was electricity, not steam, that operated the mill machinery. In the first instance, there was a large motor driving the shafting that powered a whole floor; then later, an individual motor was attached to each machine.

The mill towns, large or small, developed a character of their own, based on the local products. Built of local stone, their streets paved with stone setts, they resembled natural outcrops when seen from a distance.

East of the Pennines, Bradford came to textile prominence rather late, and it was only when the eighteenth century turned into the nineteenth that the handlooms were being phased out by the new power looms. But Bradford caught up fast. By the middle of the century, what had been a quiet little market town was a city of 100,000 people. It had also become the worsted capital of the world. Bradford had a Wool Exchange, where world prices were set. The city developed a unique 'conditioning house' for testing wool and cloth – it included a 'moth hall', for research into the depredations caused by moths. And that part of Bradford notable for the loftiest of its warehouses became known as Little Germany.

J.B. Priestley praised 'the authentic, queer, carved-out-of-the-Pennines look of Bradford'. This place was to have its brave Victorian heart destroyed by modern developments, but it retains its Town Hall and Wool Exchange, the design of which owes much to the Italians. In the central assembly room of 'Change, where the woolmen assembled, is a statue of Richard Cobden that was erected during his lifetime; it was unveiled in 1877 by John Bright, who collaborated with him in the Free Trade movement. A man who began a career in accountancy in offices within 'Change described to me its busy-ness some 30 years ago, and its subsequent decline to the point at which it is no longer used for its original purpose.

The 1950s and 1960s saw widespread changes in the mill towns of Yorkshire as a host of small mills ceased production and, towards the end of that period, extensive and often unsympathetic rebuilding of town centres got under way.

My tour of the mill country is a personal choice, based on old friendships and associations. Almost thirty years have gone by since I wrote an article in *The Dalesman* about Queensbury, an industrialised area of six thousand people at 1100 feet above sea level. In those days, the two giants, Bradford and Halifax, would have been at each other's throats but for the 'buffer state' of Queensbury and its neighbour, Shelf.

I visited the place just a hundred years after it was renamed Queensbury; it had previously been called Queen's Head, after a local pub. Here was a reminder of the speed of change once the Industrial Revolution got under way. (Nelson, a Lancashire town, is named after a local hostelry.) While some communities pride themselves on the quantity of ozone in the air, or on the number of sunny hours in the year, the people of Queensbury seemed proud of the climatic severity. I had already become aware of the name of an alpine district, Mountain, complete with Eagle Hotel, and one local farm is called Greenland. A man I met on my visit there smiled broadly when telling me that the Institute of Heating and Ventilating Engineers gave Queensbury an exposure rating of 'severe'.

The size of the population is a reflection of the importance of the mill-owners, John Foster & Son. The Fosters were to Queensbury what the Salts were to Saltaire, the Denbys to Tong Park and the Listers to Manningham. The Fosters, like Titus Salt, developed a policy of vertical integration, performing at their mill all the manufacturing processes, from the receipt of the wool to the dispatch of dyed and finished cloth. The Fosters had their own coal mines, made their own gas, manufactured their own grease and soap – and even made their own bricks!

Today, the firm is the world's largest mohair cloth producer, some 70 per cent of production being exported, directly or indirectly, from the large mill complex perched high on the Pennines. It fascinated me, on a recent visit, to discover that Fosters retain the traditional Yorkshire method of Lister combing and flyer spinning, in which the machine eliminates short fibres and vegetable matter. In the course of a century, no one has invented a more effective technique.

When I first knew Briggus (Brighouse), it was a typical Yorkshire mill town, insular in its outlook and, let it be whispered, standing out among the old Yorkshire boroughs because it featured a red rose on its coat-of-arms. The old motto, 'By Labour and Prudence', enabled a Brigguser to exercise his right to joke against authority – by asserting that Prudence was a typist in 1893! Brighouse and Rastrick (the latter lying south of the River Calder) have long had a joint brass band. Who has not heard of the Brighouse and Rastrick Band? Or, indeed, of Albert Modley, the Yorkshire comedian who was fond of singing: 'I'm t'best bloomin' blower in Briggus Brass Band'?

Those towns in the Calder Valley that made heavy cloth on the woollen principle became known collectively as the 'heavy woollen district'. Dewsbury, Birstall, Batley, Mirfield and Ossett became noted for their 'shoddy', the product of a recycling process in which soft garments and fabrics were put through a rag-tearing machine, creating a fibrous mass, from which cloth was made. The word 'shoddy', which to many signifies something inferior, is used in Lancashire for the fall-out during the cotton-cleaning process, and in Bradford for the same material derived from wool. Shoddy, though of 'middlin' quality', clothed the masses. It was invented in 1813 by Benjamin Law of Batley.

The heavy woollen district produced mantles (heavy coats) or wove blankets, though strictly speaking a blanket should not be classified as 'heavy woollen'. Two blanket mills in lively competition 'watched each other to see what was happening!' I was told. One worker in a blanket mill had an unusual experience in 1940 when he was called up into the Army to serve in the Cameron Highlanders. 'I happened to glance at the blankets they'd issued me with. I said: "Good lord! They're brown–greys. I helped to make the damn things – now I'm sleeping on 'em!"' The Yorkshire town of Dewsbury made blankets for shipping lines. 'I remember some scarlet blankets with ten different black bars on 'em; these were made for China. Somebody called 'em "Chinese wedding blankets". They reckoned those black bars on a border stood for something in their religion.'

Todmorden, on the Calder, is the focal point of three valleys, its shape resembling the three-legged emblem of the Isle of Man. 'Tod' has a border status. I once had coffee with the Mayor in his parlour at the handsome Town Hall, a gift of the Fieldens, *the* local family. His Worship recalled dancing in the Town Hall, under which flows a watercourse that was then part of the county boundary. 'I had one foot in Yorkshire, and one foot in Lancashire.'

When I was last in Todmorden – it was one December, and I arrived under the unblinking gaze of dozens of plastic Father Christmases, part of the street decoration – I managed to dodge the traffic and found a place from which to survey the classical embellishments to the Town Hall. While I was looking at the Grecian-style frieze, which I knew of old, a passing native of Todmorden pointed out something I had missed – one or two figures adorning a central plinth marked 'LANCASHIRE and YORKSHIRE'. The windows on the 'Yorkshire side' of the Town Hall are decorated with a fleece, and those on the 'Lancashire side' with a cotton plant.

Halifax, in a basin set between hills that rise to over 1300 feet, once gave the impression of being a smoking cauldron. The many busy mills made the nocturnal view of Halifax from Beacon Hill (850 feet) quite astonishing. Here where the River Calder now flows, water and ice millions of years ago created a distinctive gap, a disc slipped from the Pennines, the 'spine' of England. I'm glad that I knew Halifax before the drastic modern developments, for I loved its many Victorian buildings, which gave the impression of being held together as much by soot as by mortar. The extensive Piece Hall, recalling in its name the old-time clothiers, has never looked better and is fully used. Halifax Town Hall, of vaguely Italian style, was designed by Sir Charles Barry. At the Civic Hall the local choral society – the oldest of its type in Yorkshire – regularly demonstrates the West Riding love of good vocal music. One winter evening, I found it well worth while to cross the snow-sprinkled heights between Keighley and Halifax to attend a concert at which Vaughan Williams' *Sea Symphony* was being sung.

Halifax and Huddersfield were early developers in the textile revolution. Huddersfield, like Halifax, has also found its way into the history books through the quality of its principal choir. The Huddersfield Choral Society has become so well known for its rendering of Handel's *Messiah* that it might be said to furnish the definitive version. Huddersfield demolished its Cloth Hall in 1930, but preserved the pillars, clock tower and doorway, incorporating them in a public shelter and summer house in a local park. Like many another northern town, Huddersfield has redesigned its town centre and disciplined its traffic. In the textile context, this town has long been noted for its 'classy' worsteds.

Lancashire mill towns were once individualistic – old towns, overlain with mills and terraces and ringed by countryside. But as I motor on the M6 at night, I now tend to think of South Lancashire as being one great urban area, an impression gained from the blaze of sodium chloride lighting. Now there is no real darkness; no real demarcation between one place and another. The M6 is itself a spectacle, flanked by what appear to be gigantic strings of beads that stretch to infinity, and the towns are marked out by pools of orange light. This unreal glow makes red cars look cream-coloured, and imparts to the healthiest of people a death-like pallor. A million lights stain with orange the underbellies of passing clouds.

Manchester had a certain homeliness when I first knew it, but it is now beyond my comprehension, being so vast and varied. The Cotton Exchange no longer fulfils its original purpose. And the cotton men had their Manchester Club, at which one might well see a number of Lancashire personalities, including the artist Lowry in his crumpled suit, one end of his collar sticking upwards, and hair as tousled as a thorn hedge!

Lancashire as we knew it has, since 1974, been 'messed about' by the Boundary Commission. Of the great settlements west of the Pennines I have a special regard for Bolton ('Bowton'), which became the home of fine-cotton spinning. At Rochdale, where Gracie Fields, brought up amid the brick walls of the cotton and woollen mills, bestrode the granite setts on her way to work, the Co-operative movement was inaugurated: here twenty-eight Lancashire lads, 'the Pioneers', each subscribed £1 towards the setting up of a shop, which opened for business a few days before Christmas in 1844.

I have mentioned Accrington's former importance as a mangle-maker. This town and Blackburn, on the north-west edge of the Rossendale Fells, have played a worthy part in the story of Lancashire cloth-making. Burnley's reputation, too, is assured, not only as a notable weaving centre but also for its engineering firms. Burnley is at the edge of a conurbation that takes in Brierfield, Nelson and Colne – 'Bonny Colne upon the hill' – and then fizzles out amid the heather and sphagnum bogs of the county border.

Oldham (Owdham), the hub of the Lancashire spinning area, and Bury, the setting for an industry that was richly varied in size and range of products, were 'gradely' in the textile era. They have now diversified their industrial life.

Saddleworth, on the Pennines close to Oldham, is an unusual place, firstly because, as implied earlier, there's no actual town of that name. There's a Saddleworth Station and a Saddleworth cricket team, but the name is primarily used to cover eight quite large villages, including Greenfield, Uppermill, Delph, Dobcross, Denshaw and Diggle. 'Diggle is at the end of the famous Standedge Tunnel; when a train appeared to view, in the old days, the stationmaster shouted: "Dig'l!" All you heard was the "l".' This whole area, which used to be staunchly Yorkshire, found itself in Greater Manchester when the county boundaries were reorganised, and – according to a native – is now unsure where it lies. Saddleworth, anyway, is on the wrong side of the hill. 'You have to cross the mountain to get to the real Yorkshire, at Marsden.'

Although it is Lancashire that is particularly associated with cotton, and Yorkshire with wool, wool and cotton did not keep exclusively to separate sides of the Pennines, and both were represented at Saddleworth. One man who knows the place well recalled that, in the 1920s, when the slump led to mills being 'wiped out in their hundreds overnight', the Bradburys – already mentioned in relation to tartans – acquired a mill which had been run by the Albion Spinning Company. 'That was a case where a small woollen mill had been succeeded on the site by a huge cotton mill and then it came back to being a woollen mill.' My informant added: 'Now, by the way, it's a block of flats!'

4   The Working Day

The workers were rottenly paid. It was a tradition of the industry to pay rotten wages, though some people worked for us for fifty years.

A mill-owner

I'se nivver hed sich a job i' mi life. If yer copped [caught] sweating, yer sacked.

A mill worker

The mill drew its power from a steam engine and a huge Lancashire boiler. A story is told in one of the West Riding towns of a boiler that was delivered on a trailer drawn by a traction engine. The driver and his mate reached their destination as the workers left for their mid-day break. When the workers returned, both the traction engine and the boiler had vanished. Ere long, the sound of their return was heard. A bystander inquired of the driver where he had been. 'Nay,' he said, 'me and my mate fancied some fish and chips – and we didn't want to walk to t'shop.'

Standing near the India Mill at Darwen is a piece of machinery connected with the departed world of steam. It is a cross-compound engine, typical of hundreds that found a place in the Lancashire weaving mills from 1830 onwards. This specimen, made at Bolton in 1905, was installed in the following year at a shed containing 1224 looms.

The spinning mills needed the largest engines, which were of the vertical type, each with an enormous flywheel from which extended driving ropes, operating a shaft on each floor. The swish of ropes up the wallside created a gale inside the mill. A horizontal type of engine was sufficient for a weaving shed, the size and power of the engine being closely related to the number of looms. At Ellenroad spinning mill, near Rochdale, there still stands a 3000hp engine (see page 69). With it, in the old days, went five big Lancashire boilers. The smoke would rise up a 220-foot chimney – a Victorian colossus with extensive underground flues. Stanley Graham, who led the team that restored the engine, has described it as 'a massive monument to a lost army of ordinary men and women who gave their working lives to the textile industry'.

Ivan Parker, of Brook Shed, Earby, recalls Dennis, the last engineer of the old style, whose engine house was his pride and joy. 'I can remember when you had to knock on the door and ask permission to go in. Everything was immaculate . . . It was a showy engine, and with it went two 7ft 6in Lancashire boilers. In its heyday, the shed had 1400 looms. The engine took between 30 and 40 tons of coal a week.' The engineer, sometimes known as the 'engine-driver', saw to the running of the mill as a whole, including the steam pipes that extended the full length of the shed. 'Folk 'ud complain if they weren't warm enough.' The engineer had two fire-beaters (boilermen, or stokers) under him. 'They had the brawn. It was a pretty hard job, though at Victoria Mill, which has now been pulled down, they had *four* Lancashire boilers; it was quite a job keeping them going.'

At my home town of Skipton, I sometimes walked along the canal bank just to watch men unloading coal from barges, shovelling it into wheelbarrows which they then pushed along planks to the bunkers of Belle Vue Mill. (In attendance was Billy Gelling, who collected any spilt coal, much of it from the bed of the canal, and sold it in the town.) At Rochdale, the coal cart tipped the coal into a bunker serving the five large boilers. The fire-beater not only shovelled coal; he regulated the draught by opening and closing the dampers in the flues. Every now and again he cleaned the fires, one at a time, taking the clinker away in a barrow when he could find a moment to do it.

The fire-beater's job was demanding and ill-paid. A West Riding mill-owner told an applicant: 'I want thee here at five-thirty in t'morning; thou'll git awf-an-ahr fer thi breakfast, awf-an-ahr for thi dinner an' tha'll knock off at six.' 'And how mich do I get for t'job?' 'Twenty-five bob a week,' was the reply. 'Aw aye,' remarked the applicant sarcastically, 'an' do I 'ave ter bring mi own coil [coal]?'

You could nearly always tell a fire-beater: if he was right-handed, his left arm had no hairs on the back of it; they had all been frizzled off by the fire. You tended to hold your arm up to shield your face from the fire as you were using the rake.

'Being a fire-beater was one of the hardest jobs in the mill,' says Stanley Graham.

You opened a firebox door. The fire was burning as hot as molten steel. It burned your face and arm as you turned the fire over to one side to get at the ashes underneath. You dragged hot ashes out; you got all the sulphur fumes and there was also dust flying about. A good fire-beater cleaned up immediately. A bad man had a boiler with a front made nasty by spillage. Some boiler houses had glazed brickwork and they used to wash it down. It was kept spotless.

When Dalton Mill, Keighley, was built in the 1860s, the decision was taken to provide the power from a single unit. Into being, as noted in the Introduction, came the largest mill beam engine on record. Built by a Burnley firm over seven years, the engine cost £12,000, and developed over 2000hp. One large Dewsbury mill had a steam engine that was 'a bit awk'd sometimes':

> If they didn't stop it just reight when they knocked off for dinner, they couldn't get it to go until they'd 'barred it round'. The idea was to get the piston to the stop ready for going over. T'engineman would say – 'Gir [give] us a hand to bar this wheel over?' We'd use a great big crowbar and jam it into a hole in t'wheel, then lever it round.

Visiting Queen Street Mill at the edge of Burnley, I saw a tandem compound engine that had served the mill since the opening day in 1894. Made by William Roberts & Son, of Nelson, and one of an estimated 250 supplied to mills in the area, it has a flywheel of 14-foot diameter – which is not an especially big one – and generates 500hp. (A really big engine generates at least 1800hp.) This engine was renamed *Peace* to celebrate the end of the 1914–18 war. 'It had previously been called Prudence, after the engineer's wife,' Arthur Martin, the engineer, told me.

The engine-tenter did little else but keep watch on the machinery.– to 'tent' is to watch – and he was usually the son of a tenter, who would have been introduced to the job by his own father, also a tenter. So his knowledge of the engine came from hearing about it from his forebears and also from his own observations. He had a thankless job, being not especially well paid – despite his responsibility for keeping the mill operating by providing steam power. In some mills he worked twelve hours a day, seven days a week. The tenter was at the mill early, and he returned after the normal day's work to stoke up the boiler. At the week-end break he would bank up the fires in the boilers and do maintenance work.

Normal service was resumed in time for early Monday working. Anyone standing nearby would hear a reluctant growl from the gearing. Then the engine would settle down to its regular beat. When, in Wakes Week, the annual holiday, the mill was closed, the tenter and the boilermen had the opportunity of conducting a major overhaul.

A Lancashire boiler, some thirty feet long and with a diameter of eight or nine feet, impressed everyone by its bulk. It made good steam – and plenty of smoke. A typical boiler of moderate size had a length of 120 feet, with a diameter of nine feet and a capacity of 30,000 gallons. It had twin fireboxes and incorporated a method of preheating the water. The fuel for the boiler fire was gravity-fed from hoppers.

The most impressive of the steam power plants were those connected with the multi-storeyed Victorian spinning mills, such as Ellenroad near Rochdale, mentioned at the beginning of this chapter. The mill has gone; the engine remains to impress us by its fitness and power. It is an enormous engine, generating 3000hp and having a flywheel weighing 85 tons. It served a mill that covered 270,000 square feet – a mill built on a green field site near running water. Mill engines were extremely thirsty: up to 6000 gallons a minute were needed to keep the Ellenroad monster in action.

Stanley Graham says: 'A lot of people get a romantic notion about steam engines without actually knowing why. It's a basic thing. By using fire and water and coal – the three elements – they produced steam; they could build steam engines capable of producing unlimited amounts of power. If you didn't have enough power, you built another engine or put a second one next to it.' Such a gigantic engine drew respect from adults and instilled terror into the more sensitive children. At Brighouse,

our nearest mill – it was owned by Woods – had a beautiful engine. My daughter was scared to death of it. I used to take my children near the mill on my way to the old home in Elm Terrace. My daughter would not walk on the same side of the road as the engine. I used to say to her: 'Look – it can't hurt you. That big gate can't fall down. And that gentleman down there' – he was t'engine-tenter – 'is a very nice man who won't touch you.' But no – we had to walk on the other side of the road!

One of the mill steam engine's many admirers was a man who started work at Brook Shed, Earby, in 1948. There he became familiar with a cross-compound named *Progress*. His employers were the Kelbrook Bridge Manufacturing Company, one of five companies that hired 'room and power' from a shed company established in 1908, building 'on spec'.

Kelbrook Bridge made tartans, handkerchiefs and tie cloths, using over sixty check-looms, the rest being Cooper back-up looms, which wove satins. It was a real 'fancy' shop. The old 750hp steam engine never let us down. On Friday, my boss would tell me how many looms were running. Then I went up to the engine house and gave t'driver, as I called him, all t'particulars for t'week. The shed company then knew how much to charge.

Steam engines produced ash in vast quantities. This ash was carted away and dumped wherever space might be found. At Dewsbury, I was told that I might 'dig down anywhere round here and there's so much ash you'd think there'd been a volcano'.

At Skipton, Eller Beck – 'the stream of the fairies' – acquired rainbow hues when passing a dyeing department. In my boyhood, I had many glimpses into working mills. If a mill door had been left open, the outward rush of warm, sweet-smelling, cottony air in my nostrils impelled me to look into the shed. My eyes could take in almost everything at a glance. Good, even illumination was afforded by the 'north lights' that were a feature of the saw-shaped roof. I was fascinated by the streamlined shapes of the shuttles, made of hornbeam or American dogwood, and by the pirns (bobbins), which had been fashioned from beech. It sounds romantic – and yet the average shed was an unlovely place, with rough walls and littered work-benches, flapping belts and chattering looms.

People I recognised, some from Chapel, were among the workers; they looked grey and pinched. These little people – for there were few giants among them – had lost out in the lottery of life and were destined to spend most of their conscious life as slaves of King Cotton. The oldest remembered when weaving sheds had gas lighting, when a tedious job each morning was lighting the mantles with a taper. 'Sometimes it'd come dark, like a thunderstorm, and we had to go and light 'em up specially. When we sort of got 'em lit up – it come light again!'

Most manufacturers did not spend much brass on their premises, and informative signs or notices were rare. Push open a door and you might find yourself in an office, in the boiler house or in a warehouse. You had to try again! When the office was found, it would be spartan, with Bob Cratchit-type desks. One manager told me: 'I preferred to stand. It didn't restrict your movements as much as slumping in a chair.'

Further down the Aire Valley from the cotton belt where I was brought up, the accent was on wool, and here the stranger had to assimilate yet more textile terms. Lettice Cooper, writing in 1950, mentioned dipping into 'that cauldron of smoke' (Bradford) and seeing notices proclaiming Wool Merchants, Wool Staplers, Tops and Noils, Dyers and Spinners. Of this collection of occupations, our stranger would be most intrigued by 'Tops and Noils'. Raw wool goes through various processes, in different mills. Some of the wool is made into 'tops', which are long strands. The tops are made into yarn; the yarn is spun into thread; and the thread is woven into cloth – mainly worsted cloth if tops are involved. The shorter wool is called 'noils', and is used for rougher material.

To see lorries rumbling through Bradford transporting hessian-covered bales of wool was to witness an integral part of the old West Riding. Some of the wool had come from sheep stations under the big skies of the Antipodes and South Africa. Older folk have told me of the days when wool that had been shipped to Hull or Liverpool arrived in Bradford by rail. The wool was then transported to the warehouses, using the heavy horses and drays of the railway company.

Bradford is like Rome in that it was built on seven hills; the horses and drays presented a brave sight as they went up such a thoroughfare as cobbled Goodwin Street. At the bottom of the steepest hills were 'chain horses', attended by lads not long out of school. As a loaded dray approached, a lad hooked the chains attached to the collar of the horse into fitments at the end of the cart shafts, and off they went up the hill. Here the chains were unhooked, the lad would leap on to the horse's back and ride the animal to the bottom of the hill to await another load.

At the warehouses, the drays were parked in such a way that the wool could be hoisted directly to the open doors, high above ground level, where the bales were expertly caught and dragged inside by men in long, greasy, blue-and-white checked brats. The bales were never packed tightly together. An ingenious system of checks ensured that wool of a certain quality, from a certain source, could be found in a matter of minutes.

Ship, canal barge, horse-drawn wagon, steam-hauled train – these means of transport sustained the textile industry. The Leeds and Liverpool Canal lay at the back doors of the big mills and ensured that the transportation of coal was relatively cheap. This waterway was essentially a Bradford project, for the city raised much of the capital for it, and the company's head office remained in Bradford from the canal's opening until 1850.

The mills themselves had an impressive back-up from a variety of engineering companies. Dozens of specialist concerns had machines on offer. Hattersley looms were made in Keighley and Dobcross looms at the village of that name in the Saddleworth area. Keighley was also the setting for Prince-Smith, comb-makers. The engineers included Hodgson's of Frizinhall, Lee & Crabtree of Shipley, Briggs of Gomersal, also Hutchinson & Hollingworth of Diggle, Saddleworth.

The woollen business, as with cotton, was labour-intensive. A woollen enterprise depended greatly on the sensitive touch and quick eyes of the sorter, who distributed the different parts of the fleeces among the various skeps (or baskets); which skep the sorter chose in each instance took into account the length and quality of the wool, and the amount of fat in it. When wool cost more than sugar – as the saying goes – the floor on which the sorting operation took place was always well swept!

Baled wool, harsh and greasy, became delightfully soft and white when scoured. After sorting, the wool intended for worsteds was combed or carded into 'tops', which were taken to the drawing room. Here their density was gradually reduced until the wool was as fine as sewing cotton. There followed the spinning and weaving processes. A woman brought up in Clayton in the 1930s clearly remembers the local bleaching and dyeing mill, a branch of the Bradford Dyers' Association, 'where the creamy-coloured bolts of wool on long spindles were shrunk and dyed before being sent to the cloth manufacturers'.

The Yorkshire looms used for worsteds did not chatter as loudly as did looms in the Lancashire weaving sheds, the wool being dense and so absorbing some of the machine noise. Also, looms in the West Riding were not as closely packed into the available space as were those where cotton was being processed. In Yorkshire, orders were sent to the mill manager, who then made plans for the weaving. He would design as well, if necessary. A former director told me: 'I would say to my manager – "I want this copying; can you make me this?" Sometimes a customer would give me a pattern to work from.'

Overlooker, foreman, loom-tuner – call him what you will – this was the person who ensured that the machines worked efficiently. At Saddleworth, when there was a night shift, a mill director was in the habit of going down to the mill to ensure that all was well. He'd see the loom-tuners sitting outside, smoking their pipes or cigarettes. He would smile to himself. If they had nothing to do, everything in the mill was going well!

At Brighouse, I chatted with someone who had literally 'gone through the mill' in an area where the local products ranged from cotton cloth to carpets. Ethel, as a half-timer, dividing the working day between mill and classroom, first went to the mill in 1918 on the day following her twelfth birthday. For her labours, she was paid 2s 6d a week. 'I worked first for a firm called Woods, at the top of Beck Lane, down Thornhills. They were spinners and doublers. It was artificial silk. They put it on a warp and sent it to the weavers.' This twelve-year-old started work at 6.30 a.m. and worked until 1 p.m. one week, and in the following week started at 1 p.m. and finished at 5.30, sometimes six o'clock. There was half an hour for break-fast and an hour for dinner.

Ethel was a doffer, charged with the collection of 'cops' from the spinning frames. The cops were taken to a basket which, when full, was transported to the doublers. 'A young lady was bending down when she got her hair fast in the machinery; it scalped her. She'd had her hair tied back, but there were no caps or anything. I used to plait my hair because it was long.'

At the age of thirteen, Ethel went full-time as a spinner, having been able to leave school a year earlier than usual because she had never missed lessons; 'and I had all my marks; otherwise I would have had to wait till I was fourteen'. At the spinning mill, she had a faulty frame to use. 'It was terribly hard.' Her wage rose to 12s 6d a week. She worked in a gas-lit mill with limited toilet facilities. 'Only three could go at a time; they had "checks" hanging on a pole. If the checks had all been taken, you had to wait until one of them had been brought back.' She left this mill to become a weaver.

I had to pay £1 to the woman who was teaching me to weave. We wove linings, with patterns in them, using a jacquard loom. A coarse 'sponge cloth' was fashionable. We wove it in 108-yard lengths. You could work on what they called the 'dead horse', booking for one week's wage a piece that was in the loom at the end of the week. You got less pay in the following week!

Ethel stayed here until she was fifteen, 'and then I went to Firth's, a carpet mill at Bailiffe Bridge. My father and sister worked there. As time went on, they built a new mill up Victoria Road. Mine was the first loom to be moved to the new place.' And so she stood by a chattering loom for hours on end. Having an end down (a broken thread) was a frustrating business:

You had to pull it back till you got to the pattern again and try to match up; then you had every thread to thread back again through a series of tiny holes. That taught you not to let it run down!

If you had too many 'ends down', you had to go up to the sewer [mender]. There were some miserable sewers! They had to put all the bits back that you'd let go. If one of 'em reported you to the boss, you were sent 'up theer' [to the office] where you listened to her prating [talking sternly].

If the weaving was not acceptable, 'they cut off the piece that had all the ends missing; they sold it as "imperfect". We were never fined – though we were played heck wi'!'

When James Gregson, the playwright and broadcaster, retired to Grassington, I would call for a chat. Dick – as he was known to his many friends – was born and bred (in some poverty) at Brighouse. He started work at the mill as a half-timer when he was but twelve years of age.

The first lesson I learnt in the mill was to take punishment without squealing. One of the lads who started when I did was cleaning the machinery while it was in motion, which was against the law. A wheel ran over his bare foot and nipped off the end of his little toe. He let out a yell that brought us all running to the scene. He could hardly speak for blubbering – rocking on his bottom and nursing his foot.

The boss, losing patience with him, shouted: 'Sethee! Stop that rooarin', ye gret babby! Tha couldn't make more noise if tha'd had thi heead cut off!'

'It was sound logic, of course,' Dick observed, 'but a little insensitive.'

The feeling of camaraderie existing between overlookers and hands was fostered on the part of the overlookers by a blend of cajolery and downright, blasting sarcasm. Most boys left the mill after two or three years to take up apprenticeships. Many girls stayed on and continued twisting, winding, weaving or mending, some spending all their working lives at the same mill.

Anyone who lived handy to the mill could go home for the mid-day meal, leaving less fortunate folk to settle down in the nearest place – sometimes beside the machines – to have their snack meal, or jock. This would have been covered, for cleanliness' sake, by a clean handkerchief, either red spotted with white, or of some floral pattern. A mill worker might talk of his feeding place as a 'snap oile' or 'scalding oiles'. Presumably the last-named had a supply of steam-heated water to use for 'mashing' tea. In more affluent times a number of workers would send out to the local shops for pies or perhaps fish and chips, liberally spread with salt and vinegar.

Conditions in a mill could be nauseating. A woman working at Illingworth in the West Riding in the 1930s recalled 'an oily smell from the wool first thing in the morning. The smell seemed to go as the day wore on.' A Yeadon woman remembered the terrible sanitation, with only three earth closets for sixty women. 'All three closets were infested with rats . . . People grumbled, but they accepted the conditions; jobs were then hard to come by.' Factory lighting was generated by the engine. At the end of the day, when the engine was stopped, the lights dimmed and went out, 'so it was one big rush by the workers to get out before they were in total darkness'.

The rag-sorters of Dewsbury and Ossett – they who were engaged in the 'shoddy' business – were never quite sure of the origin of the rags. They were collected over a wide area, the dealers paying coppers for those brought in by poor people and by children. Rags were also imported. In the early days, those who were concerned with shoddy might pick up disease – or fleas. A local civic motto, *Inutile utile ex arte*, translated as 'useless things by art made useful', is quite appropriate here. There's a much better class of rag today, thanks to the washing machine and the throw-away society. But one drawback is the increasing use of man-made fibres in an industry reliant on natural fibres.

Women, known as 'girls', even though they might be of mature years, did the work of classifying rags by quality and colour prior to baling, working towards a woollen mixture or a cotton mixture. A Dewsbury rag-sorter who began a long career in 1933 told me:

> My mother and all her sisters were in it; they all went in the rags. She took me into it. There were 'rag places' all along Bradford Road. Over thirty women worked where I did. We used to sort the rags into baskets; the baskets were emptied by some boys who baled them and they used a crane to put them on to the wagon . . . for a time I used to make big 'bags' with hessian.

Shears – very similar to the hand-shears used by the Dales farmer in the old days for clipping wool from the sheep – were deftly used by the women in cutting up the rags. 'They sprung back, oppen.' In a shoddy mill, the workers were presided over by a foreman – and occasionally, a forewoman. Above the foreman, at the average mill, was the owner, 'who'd also be the management'.

The machine that made the recycling of rags possible was of a brilliant but simple design. 'My firm had a dozen "pulling" machines. The material was held under pressure by two fluted rollers. A revolving cylinder, from which pins protruded, turned at a fairly high speed, though it was varied according to the end product required. The rags were converted into a fibrous mass, which, after being 'carded', was spun into yarn.'

For many families employed in 'shoddy', it was a matter of 'from rags to riches'. Burrows, Crowthers and Blackburns were among the families who made a lot of brass. 'Offices at the biggest shoddy mills were opulent. I wish I had some of the furniture I saw there. I saw nothing but the best – solid oak.' What used to be known by the name of shoddy is now produced on an even larger scale as 'flock', to be used as padding for chairs and for bedding.

King Cotton provided his weavers with the Lancashire

loom, which was elemental: 'There was nowt fancy about a Lancashire loom; it was a reight blacksmith's job.' The principles of the loom had been well established in the days of the handloom.

The old-style Lancashire weaver can still be seen at Queen Street Mill, Burnley, where over the years the Lancashire looms have turned out a narrow grey cloth intended to be finished off elsewhere. Such cloth may look white rather than grey to a layman, but it still bears the tint given to it by the sizing process; it becomes truly white when bleached.

Queen Street, when I visited it to absorb the atmosphere and manners of a real Lancashire mill using real Lancashire boilers, had not been on full-time production for eight years. Some looms were operating, but it is now something of a showplace of the Lancashire industrial heritage. I parked my car in a capacious yard between Queen's and King's mills, in a part of Burnley where redbrick chimneys still rake the sky. Three young lads were fishing for roach in the nearby dam. One of them had half a dozen fish in his storage net. The shadow of a chimney lay across the water.

I chose a door at random and found myself in the boiler house. Cherry-red fires were visible. The air was almost too hot to breathe. Near the two Lancashire boilers, dated 1895 and 1901 respectively, was a heap of 'singles', or specially graded one-inch lumps of coal. For years it has been delivered by lorry, but originally the mill coal was transported from Bank Hall Pit, down in the valley, by horse and cart. I selected another door, and climbed steps to the engine room. After apologies for my intrusion had been accepted, I was shown the original steam engine, *Peace*, described on page 68. Then on to the main weaving shed, where all was still. Over a hundred looms, in long rows, stood unattended. A few weaving rooms had been set up in the old warehouse. I met two weavers. Were these the last of the famous lasses from Lancashire? I mused. These ladies had the traditional high spirits of the Lancashire weavers. When I requested a photograph, one put an arm around the other and they smiled and joked.

Until the 1939–45 war, the mill-owners had no worries about recruitment, for there was little diversity of interest – little to divert attention from the clattering looms. School-leavers from working-class families would 'go in th'mill' as a matter of course. Many outstanding academic careers have failed to blossom because of the limited number of scholarships and, even if a scholarship be won, the near-impossibility for many families of providing a grammar or high school student with all that was required. One Colne boy caused a sensation when he turned up at the Grammar School wearing – clogs!

Even a young person's wage was vital for the family well-being. Father would shake his head sadly and say to his lad: 'Nay – I knaws thou's bright, but thou'll hev to go in th'mill. We need t'brass.'

Textiles employed four times as many women as men. The Lancashire mill girl demonstrated many times over how the human spirit can triumph over terrible conditions. At Colne, Phil Smith – himself a native 'mill-towner' – met one elderly lady, a former weaver, who recalled the time when a week's wage was about 28s – 'Th'owd twenty-eight shillings, about £1.40 today – and that was when you were on full capacity weaving'. Only two looms might be available, 'but you'd to stand there all week. With two looms, you'd be taking home less than you'd get off th'dole. You daren't say anything. You'd got to accept the conditions.'

There was a selection process, during which the weavers looking for work would stand like a row of cattle. It helped the prospects of a 'tramp' weaver if he or she was of the same religion as the boss. It also helped if you went to the same chapel as 'th'manager, never mind boss'. At Earby, 'if somebody missed coming in to work, boss would say to one of these "tramp" weavers: "Eh – you!

Ger on them six looms theer!" That weaver would be on 'em for t'day.'

In Lancashire, the equivalent of the 'overlooker', as he was known in the West Riding, was the 'tackler'. Queen Street Mill has retained, as a showpiece, its 'tacklers' cabin', in which the tacklers of old sat, or even slept. Here there were tea-brewing facilities and a broad window through which to 'keep an eye on things'. 'A lot o' tacklers didn't like being wakkened up if they were sat on a bench, nodding off,' I was told.

Traditionally, a tackler's job was to put warps on to the looms and to keep those looms running. In the early days, he was paid according to production. It was vital for him to keep the machines operating efficiently, even if it meant occasionally having to improvise, using bits of string. The tackler – now referred to in the industry as a 'textile technician' – would 'tackle owt. They allus used to say of a chap: "Tha'll nivver larn 'im to weave; so larn him to tackle." ' In fact, a man became a tackler after being a weaver. He was familiar with every part of the loom. 'A Lancashire loom was basically a lot o' nuts and bolts. You'd hammer this and bray [pound] that. Or you'd mess about wi' a screwdriver. Now it's a lot more technical.'

A tackler must have the ability to feel for the correct delivery of cloth, and be sensitive to the proper flight of the shuttle. With the Lancashire loom, the shuttle is flung from a leather sling. 'That movement is smooth and beautiful – if all is well!' But the automatic loom of today does not have this conventional shuttle. Sometimes, the tackler had to take a defective piece of a loom along to the local blacksmith. 'A Lancashire loom was efficient if it was "tackled" right. The Earby blacksmith Harry Taylor was said to do more work for t'mills than what he did shoeing horses.'

I was told of a particularly helpful tackler who lived at Kelbrook, a village lying between Barnoldswick and

Earby. This tackler was 'a reight nice fellow,' said the man who sang his praises.

One morning, I went in to help a weaver set her looms on. It was just after engine had set off. Now I didn't shove t'shuttle up reight in box. It didn't go far enough. When I pushed knocker-on to set t'loom off, it were short o' pick, loom trapped and brought so many ends out [broken yarn]. It reight upset me. I thought: 'What's t'boss going to say about this?' So I went to see this chap – they called him Albert Dewhurst – and I said: 'Albert: I've made a great mess o' that loom.' I think I wor nearly in tears cos I was only fifteen. I thought: 'I'll get a reight roastin' over this.'

Albert said: 'Don't you worry about it, lad. I'll tek 'em up.' When he'd finished, he told me to be careful what I did in t'future. Aye – Albert took 'em up. And t'boss never knew owt about it. You don't forget them things, do you? Especially in your early days. There's so many folk waiting for you to mak a mistake. I med it up to him. If Albert ever wanted a lift wi' anything, I was there to help.

The 'girls' I had met at Queen Street Mill, seeing my camera, had insisted in the tackler being photographed – sitting down, of course, with his legs resting on a wooden buffet for comfort. He was provided with a magazine to read! This tackler was another extremely pleasant man. He was also a skilled technician, as I noted when he put pegs on to the lags of a Dobby loom, a complex task. He was good at 'fettling' a delinquent loom. He understood the old ways.

But a tackler might also be something of a tyrant. At Colne, an aspiring weaver had to catch the eye of the tackler:

If he didn't like looks on you, you didn't get set on;

you used to have to stand in t'warehouse and he'd come and have a look at you. It was so degrading. There'd be twenty, thirty, even forty standing there, and in the end it would be a young flighty bit would get work because the tackler would be able to give her a tickle. That's the kind of thing we had to put up with. I stood six months at that one firm before I got a job there.

The workers 'got their own back' at the tackler by recounting droll tales about him and his kind. It is related that one tackler, making a clothes prop for his wife, could not reach the top of it, to cut the notch for the line, and so he propped it against a wall and went upstairs, doing the work from the bedroom window. Then there was the Manchester tackler who told a friend that his daughter had taken up piano lessons. 'How's she goin' on?' he was asked, and he replied: 'Till now, she's kept to t'white notes. Afore long, she'll be doing t'black 'uns as well.'

When the tacklers were unionised, they no longer had the incentive to put themselves out. To be fair to them, a mill's smooth operation greatly depended on the skills of the tackler (or overlooker). So vital was he, that he was able to be 'sarcastic' with the master and get away with it. One tackler, commenting to his boss on a batch of yarn going through the spinning room, said: 'Ah reckon nowt to it. It's makin' nowt but dawn [broken fibres].'

The tackler was a man with an aptitude for improvisation. No two looms were alike. One would call for a heavier weight at the back, to keep up the tension, than did its neighbour. Another loom might have a peculiarity that meant it must be wedged for easy running. At Burnley, I was told: 'If a tackler wasn't working, everything was grand. If a weaver wasn't working, she was getting top rate for the job. In this business, the harder you worked, the less you earned, for it meant that, mechanically, things were going wrong.'

In the bad old days, 'steaming' a shed kept the humidity high but created an unhealthy atmosphere for the workers. The Medical Officer of Health for Blackburn commented on this custom in 1887, and in the following year the borough's health committee instituted a special inquiry. It took a year to report – and not until 1929 was the problem of 'steaming' tackled effectively and the recommendations now in force receive legal backing.

The old-time weaver was on piece rates, which varied from mill to mill and, at times, within a single mill. A uniform list of rates of pay was introduced in 1892. At that time, a round figure of 20s a week was being paid to a weaver in the Manchester area. The average wage for a weaver in Blackburn in 1906 was 19s 5d, and in north-east Lancashire in 1908 between 23s 8d and 24s. A census of weavers' earnings in 1913 revealed an average of 26s 3½d per week for a person with four looms. The average wage had risen to 31s 5d by 1936.

Wages were usually collected at the warehouse, but a Colne weaver recalled that at her shed on pay day the tackler went round with a tray on which were small tin cups, each bearing the number of a loom. Those cups held the wages. The cash was tipped into the hands of the weaver concerned.

To be 'put through the mill' was an arduous, ill-paid business. Cotton production was sustained by father, mother and whichever of the children had left school. It was considered the height of working-class luxury when mother did not need to go out to work. As with the Yorkshire woollen industry, the Lancashire mill system depended significantly on half-timers. Until 1900, eleven-year-olds might be employed in this way. The system as it applied to children under fourteen, though abolished under the Education Act of 1918, did not come into practice until 1921.

The old-time weaver – the 'lassie from Lancashire' –

operated the loom, collected weft from the store, carried pieces to the warehouse and, at the end of the day, swept and cleaned the machinery. She was clad in a blouse and long skirt, over which was spread a 'warkin' brat'. She was valued for her patience, her dexterity and speed. The tools of her trade, held in a pouch, were a reed hook, comb and scissors. During the working day she moved incessantly, this way and that, attending to one loom that had become silent, then moving swiftly to another to correct a fault. Or, if small areas of cloth had been missed in the sizing process, she would deftly rub them with tallow or soap.

If there was a 'float' (fault) in the weaving, it was wise to correct it immediately. Such a blemish would be detected by the 'cut-looker' when the cloth was examined in the warehouse. If a float *was* found during the inspection, there followed the embarrassing ritual of a weaver being 'fetched up'. A lad was sent to the shed to summon the offender. A tap on the shoulder, and the flustered woman would follow the lad to have her error pointed out. As if she needed to be told! One man 'fetched up' for bad work was dressed down by the warehouse manager, who threatened that he might have to buy the piece. The offender, terribly upset, stormed back to his loom, picked up an almost bristleless brush – which was not in the least connected with the weaving process – and said to the shed in general: 'How can anybody expect a weyver to work wi' a brush like that?'

What was a poor weaver to do if there was a large flaw in the cloth? She might resort to 'letting back' – or 'back-scratting', as it was sometimes known. This was a protracted and tedious job. But if the flaw was near the end of the piece, then the flawed part might be surreptitiously cut away.

They daren't leave it about. It was a crime to have too much waste. At some mills, they weighed it. The weaver pinched it – she (or he) just pocketed it and walked out with it. Back at home, the stuff would be put away so that no one would see it. In some cases, these little stores of 'fents' were found when the house was being cleaned out on the death of the former weaver.

A weaver, who had been sacked from one mill after another for lack of application to the job in hand, was summoned to the office at the latest mill and told that his services were no longer needed. Wishing to preserve his dignity, he replied: 'You can't sack me. I gave ower when I were coming up th'steps!'

The Lancashire weaver, working away amid the continuous clatter of several hundred Lancashire looms and in a mini-blizzard of dawn (cotton-down), overcame the problem of a noisy shed by being able to lip-read. A good weaver could converse with a friend across a shed without uttering a sound. 'Mee-mawing', as it was known, worked as fast as you could think. I was told that if I went into a weaving shed, in the days when it was fully manned, I might hear a *whooo* sound as a weaver attracted another's attention. The message would quickly spread. One weaver would say something, then pause until another nodded, signifying that the message was understood.

At Colne, the story is told of weavers who smuggled out cloth, a few yards at a time; the cloth was wrapped round the waist, under the pinafore. One girl who had taken some cloth with a distinctive check pattern made it up into a dress. She had enough left over to make a bow for her hair. Her mistake lay in wearing the new outfit at the mill's annual dance. She was sacked when she reported for work on the following Monday.

If a weaver had a baby, her husband must work a little harder in the mill and bring home extra money. Mother would go back to the loom as soon as possible and, in due course, she would instruct her offspring, especially any daughters, in the weaving skills. 'Cotton trade were run wi' women', though as far as the mill-owner was concerned it didn't matter if it was a man or a woman who stood at the loom; there was equal pay. 'A woman had to do same work as a man.'

Family service was impressive, one generation succeeding another in the same mill. 'It was a family atmosphere.' A Bolton man who rose through the ranks to become a manager discovered, managerially, 'that if I was rough with one person, I had also been rough with ten or twelve people – the other members of his family!' This is borne out at Colne, where Phil Smith, chatting to a stall-holder on the market, was told:

> You had to know who you were talking to . . . Most of th'old families run to forty and fifty people. Well, I mean, if you kick one – they all go lame! The person you're talking to might be related – perhaps a brother's wife's cousin – to the person you are talking about . . . My dad was one of ten; my mother was one of seven. So you can imagine how many relations I have. At one count-up, I had over 160 cousins!'

Poor time-keeping was penalised by a fine or the threat of having looms offered to others. A Colne manufacturer 'used to stand at t'door wi' t'watch out o' 'is waistcoat pocket.' He'd say to a late-comer: 'What time do you call this?' If a worker was not in the mill within a quarter of an hour of the start of work, he or she was sent home, sometimes for a whole day. 'At some mills, if you were late, they'd put somebody else on your loom.'

No one expected the boss to keep mill hours, though some employers prided themseves on being at the mill as the first workers arrived. One manufacturer – 'he were stern, unbending but fair' – counted his son among the workers. He was 'putting t'lad thrugh t'mill'. One morning that lad slept in, arrived late at the gate and found it locked. The gate-keeper let him in. The boss was annoyed. If his son was too lazy to get up at the right time in the morning, then he must stand outside the gates like everybody else!

At precisely nine o'clock in one Colne mill, the boss would walk slowly down the 'broad alley'. There would be a flurry of waving and mee-mawing by the weavers, anxious that everyone should know of his presence and be on their best behaviour! The boss and the tackler did not care for weavers who 'gawped'; they must get on with their work. It was nothing unusual for a new-starter at a mill to get a 'clout round t'ear' for not 'watching the work'. And the new-starter often had tricks played upon him/her. Ivan Parker recalls:

I don't think I'd been in t'shed more than a couple of days when somebody said: 'Can ter do t'funnel trick, Ivan?' At fifteen years old, you're so gullible. I asked what the funnel trick was. He said: 'I'll show tha.'

He stuck this funnel down the front of my pants. I'd to balance an old penny on my forehead. He said I could keep every penny that dropped into that funnel. I thought it was a good 'do'. I'd make a bob or two. I managed one penny, then another penny. Then all of a sudden, I felt a bit wet. While I was concentrating on catching a penny, he had some water at one side and he was pouring it down that funnel!

The mill had its fair share of characters. One weaver regularly boiled an egg in the steam kettle – the one used for 'brewing up' – and 'I've sin weavers wash their feet in t'basin where you washed your hands!' One characterful Kelbrook lady and her brother joined at four check-looms. He worked most of the hours, but she went to the mill on two afternoons, so that he could have some time off. It was not unusual to share a loom. There was also a good deal of 'sick weaving'. Women with young children who could not manage to keep up the full week would pay somebody, out of their own pay packets, to run the looms on one or two mornings, or perhaps one or two afternoons, a week.

Weavers remember the happy moments – the days on which they'd 'trim up', decorating the shed for some joyous occasion, such as a royal jubilee. 'At Christmas, you had a few trimmings up and also a bit o' mistletoe. A weaver would catch a tackler coming in at th'door and reckon to kiss 'im. I suppose a weaver allus had her favourite.' And if a weaver was to be married, then the shed was adorned by such as chamber pots and pyjamas – anything to embarrass the bride-to-be and give fun to her friends. 'If somebody was going to have a baby, then half of th'shed would be knitting for 'em.' And when the looms stopped chattering for a meal break, if someone had forgotten tea or sugar, then there would be the immediate offer of it from one of the others. 'They were a friendly lot.'

Such happy days stood out from those that were best forgotten – the winter days, when with northward-facing roof lights, a concrete floor and hardly any heating, a weaving shed was like a refrigerator. 'There was just enough heat to keep the yarn happy. Your hands got frozen. Everything about a Lancashire loom was made of iron. You could hardly tie knots because your hands were like blocks of ice.' Early on a winter's day, the light in the shed would be so poor that if a tackler was seen approaching with a new warp that had black on it, the weaver dreaded working it. 'I've known a weaver take a bicycle lamp to work with her so that she could see to take the ends up on the loom.'

And so they wove cloth throughout the long days, amid the clatter of the shed and with the belts whirring dangerously about them. The maister adjusted conditions to suit production rather than for the comfort of his workers. At times a weaver must create a micro-climate at her loom, as when the shed was too dry and the yarn in danger of breaking. She would dash some water under the loom to humidify the warp. Another day, the shed might be too humid, and the yarn so moist that it slowed down the loom.

There were amusing moments. A Nelson man, told to take a tray of poppies through the shed just before Armistice Day, walked too close to a loom. A picking-stick caught his tray, sending it and the poppies into the air. 'Th'shed seemed full o' flying poppies.' Some of them descended on the looms and were woven into the cloth!

The textile industry uses terms that are bizarre to strangers. For instance, it used to have a continuous need for 'twisters' – those who twisted a new warp on to the yarn that was left in the old set. One man, who started work 'reaching in' at 'one of t'old looms that was doing fancy work', had to have the ends ready for the weaver. He was then taught how to 'hand twist' and today is one of the few old-style twisters left in the business.

In the industrialised West Riding, towards the end of last century, some thoughtful men – a number of them connected with the chapels – sowed the seeds of social democracy through a genuine concern for mill folk and other less fortunate people of the time. Bradford had an early and long association with several of the Socialist groups from which developed the Labour Party, which began to win votes from the Liberals – who had once claimed most of the political loyalties in the mill towns.

The new unions strove for improved working conditions and greater financial rewards for their members. As far back as 1918, the Dewsbury Trades Council pressed for holidays with pay to enable people to enjoy a respite from work without financial hardship. It simultaneously asked for better houses for the mill workers.

There were grim struggles in the early 1920s, culminating in 1926 in the General Strike, when singing workers from Burnley, eager to build up support for their cause, arrived in Bradford and were invited into some of the houses for meals. One visitor was heard to say: 'I don't want the earth – just enough to live on, and feed my wife and family.' Generally, the textile workers were not very well organised or demonstrative, and in the early days of the unions a worker who became actively associated with one might be threatened with dismissal. Yet the unions continued to work valiantly to improve working conditions. As far back as 1896, when the mill workers of Barnoldswick struck and employers had imported strangers to replace the lost labour, the union spent £850 a week in maintaining the strike.

The various unions generated pride on the part of craft workers. They did their best to represent the overlookers, the twisters and drawers, the tape-sizers, the warehouse personnel, weavers and cardroom workers (spinners and cardroom workers had merged). The weavers' union at Blackburn celebrated its centenary in 1952 by taking all its ten thousand members on a day trip to Blackpool. Meals were provided at a number of restaurants, and later there was dancing at the Tower, at the Palace and also at the Winter Gardens.

Some of the men, of a studious frame of mind and with the weaving going well, would keep a book beside them at the loom and read a few lines now and again. One man began to learn Greek, by memorising ten new words every working day. And some mill workers were able to 'improve themselves' in a way that broke with the mill tradition. When Dick Gregson was seventeen years old and earning 15s a week in the mill – which meant he could make a useful contribution to the family exchequer – his stepmother, though she had only the pound a week given to her by her husband, heard him in silence when he told her of the chance he would have of an office boy's job at eighteen. After a moment's thought, she said: 'We shall have to manage, Dick. Take it!' He was free to try his wings. 'I am happy to say that she lived long enough to see, and have some share in, the fuller life she had bought for me.'

On Dick's last day at the mill, he was given a lesson in honesty. The bearded, taciturn overlooker spoke to him for only the second time in his five years there. 'Thar't leeavin' us?' he asked. 'Going into a' office?!' Dick nodded. 'Doesta know what petty cash is?' asked the man. Dick said that he did know. 'Doesta know tha'll ha' to handle it?' Dick again nodded. 'Well just keep thi fingers off it!' said the overlooker. And he marched off without another word.

5 Maisters and Bosses

He was keen o' making brass and getting forrards.
        Robert Moore, mill-owner, in Charlotte Brontë's Shirley

By gum, lad, that's a bit o' good stuff.
Woolman, greeting a friend by rubbing thumb and finger against
                                        the lapel of his suit

Quite a lot of t'bosses lived at St Anne's, so they must have bin
makking a bob or two out of their bit o' weaving, mustn't they?
                                        Heard at Colne

West Riding fiction presents the mill-owner in an
unflattering way. An author's sympathies have usually
been with the workers. The boss was the man with the
watch who glowered at them as they stumbled through
the gates into the mill yard at dawn. He was the exploiter
of labour who then sat smugly on his own special pew at
Chapel on a Sunday. He sacked men 'on the spot', and
would then be chauffeur-driven to his big house above
the soot-line on the hill.

In brief, if there was 'trouble at t'mill', it was 10 to 1
the fault of the employer.

You might get back at the boss through humour. The
tale was told of a West Riding mill-owner who, being
advised to buy a swan to keep down weeds on the mill

93

dam, found it sleeping during the afternoon. The man looked at his watch and drove the regal bird into the water. 'Tha's not bahn to sleep i' mill time,' he was heard to mutter. The reality was that there was among the boss class the usual human mix of good, bad and indifferent – though many bosses, especially in the weaving areas, were known to work alongside the lads and lasses they employed, and they knew each worker by name.

The old saying, 'clogs to clogs in three generations', was often true in north-east Lancashire and in parts of the West Riding, where a man who had a bit o' faith and brass, with recourse to a system that provided room and power for rent, rose quickly through the ranks to boss-dom. His son consolidated his gains – and the grandson, educated at a posh school and used to something better than a mucky mill, squandered the brass!

An Earby man who began work as recently as 1948, which was the sunset period for most of the family firms, told me:

My boss was a great chap. He was always at work by twenty minutes to seven every morning. He came as regular as clockwork, and he'd have settled down to some job or other when t'engine was set on at seven. He'd be there when t'engine stopped at half past five.

We'd be working, say, nine hours. He put in ten or eleven hours. This boss did all his own cloth-looking and designs for handkerchiefs, which was one of our main lines. He didn't tolerate a lot o' messing about in t'shed, but if he told you off, you could hardly object. He was working as well.

Did this worker resent the radically different living standards – the difference between his employer's detached house on the hill and his own little terraced house, where you 'couldn't swing a cat round'? He replied: 'No – we took life as it came.'

Some mill-owners were gentlemanly types who collected an honour or two and became squires of rustic parishes. One or two bought up stately homes or castles and turned them into grandiose dwellings. A few purchased land and views in the Lake District. There they socialised with the Liverpool ship-owners as they looked across Windermere at the Langdale Pikes.

But the average boss was far less pretentious. In the weaving areas, some men who began life as half-timers and then worked as weavers became entrepreneurs at the right time; they not only made brass, but kept it. Such a boss would make a point of walking around each department of his mill daily. He would have a few words with each operative, calling them by their Christian names. This was not reciprocated. The worker knew his boss by the respectful term of 'Mr'. When one retired weaver took her daughter to a mill at Colne to seek a job for her, the boss put his arm round the mother's shoulders and said to the lass: 'If tha'rt awf as good at weyvin' as thi mother wur, tha'll do.'

In the 1930s members of the Smith family, of Dean, Smith & Grace, machine-makers of Keighley, walked around the town every Saturday morning between 10 a.m. and noon. They followed the same route each time so that if any of their workers needed information about the factory, or wanted help with personal problems, they knew where help was available. And at Dewsbury, one of the directors of a large concern knew his office staff so well he teased them.

I would be sitting doing the wages, with all the money on the desk – there'd probably be a couple of bags of £5 in silver shillings – when he'd come in, pick up a bag, pull back the neck of my jumper and pour all them coins down my back!

My family knew him quite well. We lived not so far away from each other. He had a big house and we lived in a tiny house, but it didn't stop his mother popping in at the week-end to borrow a loaf of bread. It happened so often, my mother got in an extra loaf for the week-end. Once, we were all sitting down to a meal and my father said to her: 'Arter goin' ta join us?' She did.

Among the many old, well respected families of the West Riding textile industry were the Denbys and Amblers of Bradford, the Crowthers of Marsden, the Taylors of Batley, the Hirsts of the Colne Valley, the Crossleys of Halifax, the Fosters of Queensbury (already mentioned) and the Craven family of Keighley. Men like the Bunzls made a mark for themselves in the 'shoddy' world of the Dewsbury district. Add to these the mighty Salts of Saltaire and the Listers of Manningham, one of whom became the first Lord Masham, and you have as shrewd a collection of businessmen as might ever be found in such a limited area.

It was a similar story in Lancashire. There were families, not all of whom were of the old county stock, who sprang into prominence as the Industrial Revolution gained momentum; soon they were dominating whole towns, to the extent of employing most of the people and providing the public amenities that the Victorians enjoyed. The mill town bosses of the expansionist period assumed the manner and stance of minor royalty.

West Riding woolmen were at their sartorial best in late-Victorian times when they attended High 'Change – the Bradford Wool Exchange. Some two thousand woolmen, meeting on Monday and Thursday afternoons, conducted international as well as local business. These grave-looking men with flattened vowels and minds as keen as razors were concerned with every aspect of the industry, not just the raw materials. If anyone had anything at all related to textiles in mind, then a few short conversations at 'Change would put the work in progress.

Each section of the trade was associated with a specific part of the floor of 'Change, its position being located in relation to the marble pillars. Woolmen – and, indeed, the Manchester men in attendance at the Cotton Exchange – knew every fine detail of textiles and were quick on the uptake when there was 'a bob or two' to be made. A fair amount of guile attended their dealings but, generally, a man's word was his bond. Thousands of pounds changed hands with little more than a handclasp to seal a bargain. John Reddihough, who died in 1924 and was one of the last to sport a top hat at 'Change, was known as Honest John through his strict adherence to his word.

The men at 'Change prided themselves on their business acumen, which enabled them to reduce normal risks to the lowest possible level. They were noted for the speed with which they made 'brass' and the tenacity of their grasp once it was secured, though stories were told of the few impetuous types who made fortunes overnight – and lost them the next day.

The most important annual flutter at Bradford concerned the purchase of wool. The season for buying ended in Australia in March, so the mill-owner had to reckon on the state of the trade in the following August. He invariably got it right. He and the West Riding prospered. In the heyday of wool, Darley Street in Bradford was nicknamed the Bond Street of Yorkshire because wealth was so much in evidence. It was claimed that every other vehicle to be seen there was a Rolls Royce.

Woolmen entertained important customers at the Midland or the Great Northern. They had their short, gruff conversations at Brown Muffs or Collinson's. The last-named restaurant exuded on to the pavement the tantalising smell of roasted coffee, tickling the nostrils of passers-by. Also at Collinson's was a trio of instrumentalists, playing the popular airs of the time. Bradford had, if not a cosmopolitan flavour, then one that was distinctly European. Henry Hardy, whose family had arrived in the city from an obscure mid-European town, established a Continental-style restaurant at which he conversed with his customers, who came from textile centres overseas, in French, German or Spanish. And, as mentioned earlier, one prominent area of the city was dominated by the warehouses and offices of 'Little Germany'.

Bradford was an exciting city to explore. There was plenty of muck and, for some, there was money. One old rhyme had it that Bradford was noted for cash, Halifax for dash and Huddersfield for show. Tales are told of the bluff and forthright West Riding 'wool barons', one of whom, one day entering the bank above which was his range of offices, said to the manager: ''Enry, ah want an overdraft.' 'Yes, sir – how much?' was the reply. 'Three quarters of a million, 'Enry, and if ah don't get it, ah'll shut b . . . bank down.' This man and a friend dabbled in anything that offered a return on their money, even financing shows on the London stage. Woolmen who could be mean over some matters were generous over others. In the 1914–18 war one of them converted his home into a convalescent centre for officers, and bought a charabanc in which injured war heroes could go out and about for the day.

Many a boss prided himself on living close to the mill whence came his brass. One such family was the Tophams at Brighouse. An office worker in the days of not so long ago told me: 'The boss's house was next to the mill. When Mr Topham died, we had to go and see the body. It was the first dead body I'd looked at. I went cold. For two days I couldn't get warm.'

Few of the new-rich could resist the temptation to build a house, away from the mill. Big detached houses appeared in quiet districts at the edge of town, or – in the case of some Bradfordians – at places like Baildon, overswept by moorland breezes. A Batley manufacturer was asked by the architect which aspect he wanted. He replied: 'Gie me one more than t'other chaps have got.'

Woolmen bought themselves mini-mansions in the lower reaches of the Yorkshire Dales. J.H. Denby's interest in Dales sheep led him to help to establish an association that fixed a type to which the Dales-bred sheep would conform. In 1930, Denby and some of his farmer friends broke the world record for transforming wool 'from the sheep's back to the finished suit'. Some Americans had accomplished this feat in six hours. Denby provided overnight accommodation, and the farmers, using the mill yard, first clipped the wool from two Lonk ewes and six Swaledales. Then the fleeces were promptly taken indoors. Three hours and twenty minutes later they had been converted into a suit.

Another dalesman by adoption was Theodore Taylor, of the Batley firm of J.T. & J. Taylor. For many years, until his death at over a hundred, Theodore commuted between Batley and his home at Grassington. It was here, when I was working as a reporter at the *Craven Herald and Pioneer*, that I met him on the day he became a centenarian. There he was – small, dapper, grizzle-grey and amazingly lish (agile) for one of his years. It was long before the days when journalists began to move about in packs, but so compelling was Theodore Taylor's birthday I found myself in a short queue waiting to interview him.

An American photographer took ages to fit up his lighting units. There seemed to be dozens of flash-bulbs, and he had a most impressive camera on a tripod. The subsequent flash seemed to light up half the village, and Theodore doubtless had purple vision for a while through the searing of his optic nerves. Next in line was a *Telegraph and Argus* photographer – a man every bit as characterful as t'photographer in Priestley's play, *When We Are Married*. He had a battered plate camera – the type known as a 'press camera' – and from it protruded a fitment holding

a single large flash-bulb. 'Nah then, Mr Taylor, let's have
a nice smile,' said the man from the *T. and A.* Theodore
obliged. The picture was taken and the camera put to one
side. I noticed that the reflector for the flash-bulb had
originally been part of a Heinz baked bean tin.

I made much in my article of Theodore Taylor's bene-
volence towards the workforce at his mill. He had introduced a profit-sharing scheme at a time when few such
schemes existed. (Unfortunately, years later, the scheme
failed. People who took shares did not benefit from them
because of a decline in value).

Late-Victorian and Edwardian mill-owners did not stint
themselves. The spacious two-storeyed houses that they
built themselves had anything up to five bedrooms, and
attics for the servants, who were expected to carry buckets
of coal to replenish roaring fires in rooms that seemed a
mile high. Every bedroom had a fireplace, which caused
draughts. At a house in Saddleworth, 'we had central
heating of a kind. We never used it because it was inef-
ficient. The house was bitterly cold in winter.' An old
friend recalls the home of a woman who inherited great
wealth from textiles. Her house continued the charm and
deportment of the mid-Victorian period well into the
twentieth century. The beds, six feet broad, were fitted
with mattresses of swan's down. Meals were taken at a
refectory table, covered by an Irish damask cloth. The
quality of furnishings would have made an antique dealer
faint with sheer enthusiasm.

The only time I had a meal in a mill-owner's house was
when I was conducting the harvest festival services at
Bradley, the little village near Skipton where Grandfather
had settled, where he worked – and where, in due course,
he was sacked by the mill-owner, almost certainly for
union activities. (But there was no subsequent rancour
between the two men.) After the service, I was invited to
have tea with the mill-owner and his second wife, Jessie,
a most delightful person. The house, in an upper part of

the village, was a working man's dream of heaven, being large, peaceful and sumptuously furnished, with an oak table spread with the whitest of cloths. The gleam of silver – real silver – cutlery caught the eye in the sun.

The mill-owner's interests were everywhere apparent – in the Bible on its oaken lectern, a gift of the Rural District Council on his retirement as a councillor, and in the neat pile of literature concerned with the United Nations and the Temperance Society. This mill-owner was a great Temperance advocate. (Unhappily, he had an ailment – unrelated to drink – that empurpled the blood vessels of his nose and led others sniggeringly to suggest that he drank in secret.) The splendid meal was eaten at a pace conducive to good talk – a pace measured by the mellow ticking of a long-case clock. Here was the mill-owner who had sacked Grandfather, and now the grandson was enjoying, through his hospitality, some of the blessings of a successful life in textiles. The wheel had turned a full circle.

One of the big textile families of the West Riding, the Fieldens of Todmorden (mentioned earlier), gave to the town a school of art, a Unitarian church of great size and beauty costing £53,000, and a town hall (opened in 1891). Sir Francis Crossley, of carpet fame, handed over to Halifax the land for its People's Park. And the Fosters bestowed on Queensbury a capacious Victoria Hall and heaped brass on the parish church. Bosses were, by and large, good to the Nonconformist causes. One impulsive mill-owner who moved to Eldwick, near Bingley, and saw that the Methodist chapel was only of modest size, promptly said: 'We'll have a bigger and better place . . . I'll pay half t'cost.'

On the other hand, Billy Grimshaw, of Blackburn, was frugal. He did not permit his chauffeur to drive his Rolls Royce at more than 25mph. He was a patriotic Lancashireman who, when new looms were purchased, gave a hand in the yard in breaking up the old looms with sledgehammers. Billy did not want them to be sold second-hand to overseas competitors, to the detriment of trade in his native Lancashire. And frugality was also a characteristic of the topmaker living in a village near Bradford, who employed his native instinct for 'makking brass' by taking surplus eggs from his hens to sell to his workers. Once, as he waited for a train, an egg rolled from an overfull basket and cracked on hitting the platform. He went into the station office to inquire if they had a saucer, with which he could scoop up the egg, muttering: 'It'll poach.' That man died a millionaire.

Stanley Jeeves, a man of humble beginnings, who was a champion of the Council for the Preservation of Rural England in Lancashire as well as being a most accomplished photographer, told me a story of a Nelson mill-owner who had a posh house on the hill. When that house was cut off after a heavy fall of snow, he rang up the mill office at 7.15 a.m. and told the office boy to ask the manager (when he arrived at 8.00 a.m.) to get thruppence from the mill safe. The boy should then collect a shovel from the engine house and use the money to travel by bus to the nearest point to the boss's house and there clear the drive so that he could get out and go to work. The boy slaved away and cleared the drive. The mill-owner did not offer him a lift to the office. He simply said: 'Thee catch t'bus with that three-orpence tha's got left.'

I have referred to the Yorkshire woolmen gathering at High 'Change, and briefly to their counterparts west of the Pennines, the Manchester men, who attended the Cotton Exchange in some style. They would be driven to the railway stations in fine carriages and, later, in fashionable chauffeur-driven cars. The ordinary folk could only gawp and marvel that people could have so much money. In Nelson and Colne, where cotton was the main commodity but some wool was processed, a manufacturer or his representative might attend both Exchanges.

The Bolton area produced textile men of somewhat gentlemanly manner. A case in point was Sir Ben Dobson, of Dobson & Barlow, manufacturers of textile machinery. Sir Ben was a cultured man, keen on literature and science. He was also a good businessman. He kept abreast of modern developments and sold his machines at moderate prices. Close to Manchester were to be found some very different textile men, the archetypal bosses – the sort the playwrights had in mind. They made no effort to improve their cultural life, they were careless in their behaviour, they flattened and broadened vowels with the best. The same applied to many of the weaving bosses of north-east Lancashire, who could also be very stingy.

In the late 1920s, the owner of a small firm at Colne did well out of commission work and was able to live at a large house on the edge of town. Yet he walked to work. He appeared to despise his workforce, and usually turned down any appeal for increased wages. When one weaver complained of poor-quality yarn, and said that before she wove any more she would gie ower (hand in her notice) first, he replied: 'Tha wean't. Tha can't afford to gie ower.' He was right. This woman was the family's only wage-earner. Her father had left home and her mother was ill.

The average boss wanted to appear prosperous in the eyes of the townsfolk without being considered 'showy'. Some whose businesses were in East Lancashire distanced themselves from the workers by catching the evening train to Blackpool; it departed from Colne at about 4.30 and arrived at its destination by six. 'Quite a lot o' t'bosses lived in smart houses at St Anne's [near Blackpool].' A story related by B. Bowker, the author of *Lancashire under the Hammer* (1928), concerned a weaver who, in 1908, married the daughter of a manufacturer, sold yarn at a half per cent commission on 'Change, became an independent yarn agent, and in 1912 moved to a fine house at Southport. By 1920, he had made £150,000 and had bought a yet bigger house at St Anne's.

A middle-aged man who in 1920 kept a small shop decided to enter the cotton trade with money bequeathed to him by his father. The village schoolmaster taught the budding businessman the rudiments of mathematics. He became master of six hundred looms, and soon afterwards began a leisurely Indian summer of retirement with £50,000. He was lucky. Within a year or so, trade suffered a disastrous decline.

Generally speaking, up to the 1914–18 war, life could be quite good for small-town bosses. A mill town community had, at the peak of its social pyramid, the boss; then there were the magistrate, the doctor and the policeman. A schoolteacher was a little lower down, on a par with ministers of religion (who were rated much more highly in rural areas). At the bottom of the pyramid was what Stanley Jeeves once described to me as 'the grey mass of working people'.

Not everyone craved a villa on the Lancashire coast, though. Amos Nelson, who started work in a mill as a half-timer and who throve mightily, bought and developed the estate of the Roundell family at West Marton. He had the old hall demolished and instructed no less a person than Sir Edwin Lutyens to design him a new one, complete with lodges. (In fact, Sir Edwin had met the wealthy Lancashire mill-owner and his wife when they were cruising, and had persuaded them to ask him to design a house. Friends warned Nelson to keep a tight rein, for Lutyens was known not to mind spending other people's money.) The new Gledstone Hall followed a favourite theme of Lutyens, and had a roof like an old English barn. Among its features is a grand staircase with alternating white and black marble steps.

The Hindleys of Nelson also achieved high social distinction; they entered the cotton trade at the time of greatest opportunity. Harold and Arthur, the eldest of three brothers, had their first experience of textiles while working for Samuel Holden, the Barrowford weaver. Having learnt the trade, they soon began on their own account, this being in 1912, during one of the mini-booms. Little capital was needed because of the 'room and power' system. They rented a shed for a reasonable sum. Soon they had two – the Vulcan Shed and the Eagle Shed – in operation.

Raw cotton from India and America arrived at Liverpool Docks, was spun at places further west and, through dealings in Manchester, was soon available to the weavers of the north-west and parts of the West Riding. The Hindleys experienced a quick turnover of money as cotton yarn was woven into shirtings, sheetings and dress fabrics. Profits were ploughed back into the business. Extra weaving sheds were rented or spare capital exchanged among the family, according to the tempo of the trade. The Hindleys' objective was to buy the premises they rented, and this was soon achieved.

Harold, a far-sighted man, felt that the future lay with artificial fibres, not cotton. He was also optimistic about the prospects for multiple stores such as Marks and Spencer and British Home Stores, which were then in their infancy. His investment in BHS laid the foundations for future prosperity. His son, John Hindley, who had been an infant when the family business was started, had undertaken a world tour and could thereby take a broader view of textiles. Harold lived for many years at Moorlands, Blacko, where in due course an extraordinary enclave was established – five large houses in a row, each family related to the others. All the brothers-in-law and sisters-in-law mixed socially, although owning firms that were trade rivals.

The Hindleys prospered. Arthur married Samuel Holden's elder daughter Beatrice, and they lived for most of their married life at Read Hall, near Burnley. John Hindley, who became a director of Hindley Brothers, set up home at Sawley Lodge, by the Ribble. Val Cutter, his daughter, relates that he caused a 'nine days' wonder' in the family by marrying a dynamic raven-haired girl from Wales in the days when local marriages were preferred, especially when they led to an amalgamation of prominent textile families!

I knew a number of the old-time bosses. Mr Pickles, of Barnoldswick, who became a director of a local mill, walked about the town very self-consciously because he felt he must wear the mark of his status – a bowler hat. Apart from his accomplishments at the mill, he was a mechanical genius who need only look at a machine to be able to remember it in such fine detail that he could copy it on his return home.

Some of the manufacturers made names for themselves in rural pursuits. I am not just thinking of the hunting field. William Cecil Slingsby, of Carleton near Skipton, was a leader of British mountaineering. He climbed in Switzerland, and enjoyed his greatest triumphs in Norway, which in his day was almost unknown to British visitors. There he revived an interest in skis, and he was the first man to take Norwegian skis to the Alps and teach the locals how to use them.

Blackburn Holden, cotton manufacturer of West Craven, was often seen in scruffy clothes; he was passionately fond of pot-holing, as underground exploration is known in the district of the Three Peaks, where there are big open shafts. None is more impressive than the main chamber of Gaping Gill, on Ingleborough. The distance from a lip of limestone to the shingly floor of the chamber is 340 feet. This was the time when pot-holers lugged around hempen ropes, and rope ladders with wooden rungs. Blackburn Holden, naturally, had his ladders made of cotton. On one occasion he successfully reached the bottom of the Gaping Gill shaft, but when the time came to return to the surface, such was the elasticity of the cotton when wet that he had to 'climb' about twenty rungs before he actually left the ground and could make the long ascent to the surface!

In the 1930s, the concept of a boss changed. Private firms were amalgamated and became public companies. Many closed down when the government offered cash incentives. The large houses became something of an embarrassment at a time when small-to-medium housing was preferred. A Saddleworth man told me: 'When my parents died – it was in the late 1950s – I sold a big, beautiful house with great difficulty and after twelve months of advertising. It really was big, and there were huge grounds. I was glad to get it off my hands. It went for £4,500.'

6   Home Sweet Home

Mother said: 'Pay as you go on. If you can't afford chairs, sit on orange boxes.'

A Lancashire housewife

We'd no such thing as carpets. We brayed [pounded] a piece o' sandstone and scattered sand on t'floor. Twice a week, we'd sweep it up and put some fresh sand down.

A former mill worker at Colne

The terrace in which I was born took its name from a famous politician, Gladstone. It was otherwise unremarkable.

Ma said you got a nice class of people in Gladstone Street. Here was the head of a Catholic school, a railwayman who slept by day and worked at night, a tweedy gent who kept sporting dogs and snared rabbits, a man who repaired shoes in his cellar, and another who – a neighbour reported – had 'summat to do wi' t'council'. And, of course, there were retired folk – like Grannie, mother's mother, ensconced at No. 1. She presided over family and friends with the regality of Queen Victoria, whom she resembled, being small and dumpy. Grannie was at her least regal, though, when smoking. She sometimes 'fancied' a cigarette. The nicotine gave an orangy hue to her top lip.

Ma told us that Grannie had come from a well-to-do family at Melton Mowbray in Leicestershire. Most families made this sort of claim, to imply they had experienced better days. Grannie must have slipped a few notches when she married Grandfather, though his father had been a schoolteacher – a headmaster, indeed. For Grandfather's greatest talents were not connected with industry. He merely put up with it, saving his best efforts for the sports field; he and his brothers excelled at Rugby and cricket.

No. 9 Gladstone Street was, as terraced houses go, 'not so bad'. It was at least a 'through house', dating from the late nineteenth century, which was somewhat better than the ubiquitous back-to-backs to be found in large numbers further down the Riding. In some houses, the front door opened straight into the living room and visitors did not seem to worry about all t'muck they trailed in.

The back-to-back house, two up, two down, was so small there was no private toilet, simply one of a row of 'closets' at the bottom of the yard. Some of them were 'tipplers', which were noisy, giving straight access to the sewer. Small children were haunted by fears of vanishing for ever. The newspapers were recycled, being cut into small squares and strung for use in the toilet. Making toilet-packs was a regular week-end job in back-to-backdom.

Our house had a diminutive front garden, a mating ground for cats. In the back yard, Ma hung out the best of the washing. Second-rate stuff was draped from lines stretching across the back street. We were discouraged from playing in the front street but had the run of the back, where the uneven stone setts, which were a hazard to the elderly, caused many a bruised or gashed knee among the careless young. Those setts did offer a sporty course for taws (marbles), though. It was a major disaster if the most prized type of marble – a 'blood-ally' – overshot and went down a drain. On washday, the central gutter periodically filled with soapy water as someone emptied a tub. Monday was a good day for the ancient sport of matchstick-racing!

The back street echoed to the cry of the ragman or the shriek of a houseproud woman who had seen the coalman walking near her freshly washed sheets. Always there was the yodelling call of a mother to her young, reminding him/her that it was meal-time or bedtime. Disobedience led to the painful business of getting t'strap.

The strap, used to inflict corporal punishment in the days when children were 'seen but not heard', was hanging by the fireplace and doubtless originated as a length of belting from the mill, giving added depth to the common expression, 'If you don't behave, I'll belt you!' Or a father might threaten to 'leather thee'. If it was left to mother, she would soften towards the miscreant. 'I hit t'bedroom steps a lot more than I hit them kids, though if they got me really upset, I hit everyone in sight. Then I was bound to get t'right 'un. Our Colin said: "I've had many a leather I never earned."'

We had a living room, a diminutive kitchen, and a front room with a bow window, which in the mill town context was something special. This room had the best furniture, the cleanest wallpaper, the smartest lace curtains and an all-pervading chapelish tang of damp books and furniture polish. Most front rooms were little used and in winter achieved the coldness of a tomb.

The best rooms were fitted with gaslight. At ground level, the illumination came from gas mantles. A bedroom had simply a bracket, with a blue flame at the end; this served to heat as well as illuminate the room on winter evenings. The lighting of the gas was a magical moment. It happened just before the curtains were drawn at the edge o' dark. I heard the hiss of escaping gas as the tap was turned; then a lighted taper was placed near the mantle. There followed a *whoosh* and a glow attended by a steady hissing sound.

The bedroom walls were adorned by reproductions of pictures of idealised children. They looked so clean, so respectful. For a fire to be lit in the bedroom someone must be ill, for it was the height of luxury. Our next-door neighbour, spurning the stone hot-water bottle, warmed her beds with an oven plate she removed at the last moment and wrapped in a blanket.

Above the small bedrooms – and unlit by gas – was the attic, where time stood mustily still, as in an Egyptian tomb. I had a fanciful idea that some long-dead body lay behind the heaps of unwanted objects and rolls of surplus wallpaper that 'might come in for something one day'. Here, too, were sepia photographs of solemn-faced ancestors, and also a tin trunk, attaché cases with burst locks, and a large vase which had held the family aspidistra. I recall the plant as one whose leaves were reverently anointed with cold tea once a week. The plant went off-colour, rejected all attempts at rejuvenation, and was even given a dose of Grannie's cough medicine, to no avail. Perhaps it died of boredom.

The stone-flagged cellar, which my youthful imagination populated with dragons, held the impedimenta of washing-day – mangle, wash-tub, dolly stick and gas-heated boiler. Here, too, was a heap of coal, which was replenished in a spectacular way. The coalman would arrive in the back street, and remove a grate above a chute-like entrance to the cellar. News of his visit having been received, a large dust sheet was put in position and the sacks of coal were poured in, one after another. In dry weather, dust seemed to hang in the air for the rest of the day.

Terraced houses came in many types, ranging from those built by speculators, the terraces forming a rigid pattern in the newer parts of town, to the rows of 'tied' houses owned by the mills and, generally, populated by a grateful tenantry. The mills ruled the lives of those operatives who were also tenants. At Lockwood near Huddersfield, before the 1914–18 war, women worked in the mills as weavers, winders and menders. It was not uncommon for menders, after marriage, to continue to work in their own homes. To the houses were taken the pieces (each a rolled length of sixty yards of cloth) needing skilled attention. They were subsequently collected by the firm, and the women were paid for their efforts on the spot.

In the beginning, life could be squalid. As a mill town entered its period of lusty growth, many a street was no more than eight feet in width, and devoid of sewers. The 'night soil' men came stealthily after dark to empty the outside privies. At Saddleworth, 'we had the usual mill cottages. They were stone-built cottages, in little blocks – one block of four, one of three'. After the 1939–45 war, when the mill company proposed to put in bathrooms at a cost of £250 per house, the tenants were asked if they would pay a shilling a week extra on the rent. They protested, but subsequently relented. 'They all liked it when it was done, you know. They now had hot water for a bath and they had an indoor lavatory.'

Most of the property was rented. The rent-collector made his doleful rounds and settling up with him was given top priority. Mother was waiting with open hand on pay-day and father, plus any children who were working, handed over what they had earned. It was mother who apportioned the available money to cover overheads and who then handed out any spending money, including that needed by the husband when he set off for the club for 'a pint'.

Solvency was another word for respectability. A woman who commented of a neighbour that 'she has nowt' would speak with some scorn, especially if that woman had 'frittered her money away'. Daughters followed their mothers in being good housekeepers. Said one: 'I wouldn't be able to get to sleep at night if I owed a lot o' money.' Another remarked: 'My mum would kill me if I got into debt.' I heard of one woman who did get into difficulties. 'She daren't tell father. She was getting stuff and couldn't pay for it. And we children were all little, so she couldn't go out to work. Oh, she were in a mess!'

Thrift was a vital necessity. 'We were taught to pay cash for everything. The rent came first because you must have a roof over your head. Then you needed coal for cooking and for keeping you warm. The next necessities were food and your gas. What you had left you could "play around with".'

A family at Brighouse rejoiced over their good fortune in having an additional bedroom, the house extending over a passageway. In the 1920s, the father, mother and five children had a living room, but no kitchen; three bedrooms, two attic rooms and a cellar. In 1931, a rent of 6s a week was paid for a terraced house in Brighouse. 'We set off with £2 a week in wages. We had things given – a table, some buffets, a tub and posser and a rubbing board . . . My sister said to me: "Always pay your rent; always pay your insurance; and never buy anything unless you have enough brass." So I never owed a half-penny rent all my married life.'

A woman who, in later times, got a 'two up, two down' terraced house in Zion Street, Colne, listed the furnishings she and her husband could afford to buy – a carpet square, two fireside chairs ('brand new; we had no second-hand stuff'), a dining room suite, and linoleum to go round that room. 'You put your lino round and polished it once a week. Every other day, you flicked the dust off with a long mop.' This woman had a gas boiler; it was used for heating the water needed for the weekly wash. 'You lit it underneath. You stuck a taper down – then jumped back six feet before the gas went *whoosh*! You waited till the water was hot and then you put in your whites, to boil 'em.'

A Blackburn couple, married during the General Strike of 1926 and fearful of getting into debt, had their first home in rooms over a grocer's shop. They had little else but a bed, a long form and a table. 'We finally got into debt by getting a desk and a tallboy; we paid for 'em at the rate of five bob a week.'

Slightly better off were the Hartleys, of Colne, who had a cottage and £150 in the bank. Robert Hartley asked his lady-love: 'Would you like to get married?' 'Yes,' she said, 'I would.' He said: 'Well, I've got just £150 in the bank.' 'I haven't sixpence,' she confessed, but it did not matter to him that she had no financial means. After their marriage, they paid £19 for a solid oak bedroom suite made to their specifications by Messrs Dean. They had a three-piece suite in Rexine, 'which was just coming out then'. The house stood at the edge of the town. Its fame spread. At week-ends, people walked over to have a look at it. 'Go and have a look at Bob Hartley's house,' someone would say, 'you've nivver sin nowt like it; it's lovely.'

Generally, though, furnishings were sparse, partly because there was so little room. Early this century, the living room of a working-class home would hold a deal table, 'on which you did everything, from scrubbing clothes to baking', also wooden chairs and a couch. 'It wasn't much. Folk today would call it "cheerless".' A terraced house in a community near Rochdale is recalled as it was in 1929 by a woman who visited it in girlhood. That house was the home of an auntie and uncle. It was 'two up and two down' – just two big bedrooms, one big living room, one big kitchen with a stone sink and a yard with a small toilet building.

The living room was furnished with a table, covered by a cloth 'with bobbles on', and a sideboard. 'There was also a plant-stand with legs that splayed out – and an aspidistra on top!' Most people in that terrace had their meals in the large kitchen, 'but my auntie was a bit posher; she didn't work in the mill. Her husband was a clogger. She always served meals in the living room. She liked to show off her three-piece suite.' The kitchen was fitted with a fireplace combining oven and water-boiler, and a stone sink with a single tap, from which issued cold water. There was a pegged rug and plain chairs. A copper, for washday, stood in one corner, and the old mangle was in the cellar. A typical bedroom held, apart from the bed, a dressing table (with jug and basin) and a wardrobe.

Bedrooms were usually spartan. The old 'uns spoke of the days when in a poor family there might be five to a bed, the sleepers being arranged tops to tails. A Burnley man remembers when, with a shortage of bedding, they were covered with brown paper which 'crinkled' all night. Patchwork quilts were popular; they could be made at home out of odds and ends of material from clothing. At Colne,

> someone gave us a bed. I'd always wanted a bed that was black, with brass knobs. This bed had been painted green! We had a straw mattress given. It had a lot of fleas. I helped my mother to bray [pulverise] camphor balls, and we sprinkled them in the mattress . . . We were poor; we couldn't afford wallpaper. One holiday, mother whitewashed over the old paper in the bedrooms.

An old lady living in the Spen Valley talked of her upbringing in a house with a riverside location. The cellar was so wet, it could be used only for the storage of the tin bath. The occupants of the house knew that the river was rising when they heard the clang of the bath as it was lifted from its hook by flood water.

Normally, a zinc bath, which had been hanging from a hook driven into the back wall of the house, would be brought indoors and set before the living room fire – a searing coal fire, the best of the week, for it was also used to heat the adjacent boiler and the kettle that would warm up the replenishment bath water as child succeeded child in the soapy swell.

I remember the pleasure of sitting in warm bathwater, a feeling of contentment that was prolonged when I got out and sat beside the living room fire, waiting for my hair to dry while watching the fantasies of white and red light, the glowing caverns and the curling smoke, amid the dark pieces of crackling or spitting coal. Friday night was also nit-hunting night, if there had been a scare at school that nits were on the rampage. Ma used a small toothcomb, which she would run through my hair. She held a white plate against my neck. When a nit fell on the plate and became as conspicuous as a red blob in a desert, she would crack it with a thumb nail.

At Colne, I heard from a native, 'we'd a tin bath. Friday night was bath night. The children went through the water in turn. When we were old enough we went to the public baths. Then it was fun keeping clean!' Bath night was also clothes-changing night. For girls, it was a time of liberty bodices and flannelette, which kept chills at bay until, when May was out, a clout might be cast in favour of a summer frock. A Brighouse woman told me:

> My husband used to bath the kids. He washed their hair. They were blonde, so they shone like anything when he'd finished. I lifted them out and dried 'em. If they were big enough, they dressed themsleves; if not, I dressed 'em. We had a bath in front of the fire till we were older. I had a clothes horse [see page 118], with a blanket over it, so that nobody could see 'em. Later, they had a bath in t'kitchen. I put the gas oven on – for warmth.

At night, the fire was 'banked up' with coal slack. The first person to rise in the morning plunged a poker into the black mass and riddled the ashes. Soon a cheerful fire was evident.

In the General Strike, the shortage of coal caused many difficulties. One Colne couple, marrying in that year, did not buy any coal until the strike was over: they wanted to support the miners' cause. Every house had a coal range which heated the fireside boiler and the oven. Without coal, a family could not even have a pot of tea. Families living not far from pit areas spent hours scavenging for coal on the pit heaps. A coal fire was the focal point in the living room. Here people sat for warmth and here flat irons were heated up for the weekly ironing. Some women spat on the base to test the heat. A protective container was clipped on to the base of the iron once it was hot. 'I had an iron you had to light with charcoal; you blew it with bellows till you got it going.'

The man of the house might relax of an evening with his stockinged feet on the high steel fender, despite his wife's lament that 'I've only just polished it'. She also polished her two sets of fire-irons – the steel set which was in use during the week and the brass set that appeared in all its gleaming magnificence for the week-end.

The housewife was quick to intercept anyone who was about to use the poker to stir up the fire. A poker was only to be used to riddle the bars and clear away the ash. Now and again, a chimney 'set on fire'. What became ignited was the accumulation of soot; from the chimney billowed a cloud of dark-grey smoke, with bits of glowing soot mixed among it. Another time, the air resounded with anguished cries as, without warning, there came a fall of soot that clogged the fire and formed a fine black drift over the tab (or pegged) rug. The chimney-sweep would be summoned and the youngest daughter kept away from school so that she could be at home to help when the sweep had done his work. 'And think on, love, don't let 'im go till you see t'brush sticking out of t'chimla'.'

Cleaning soot from the tab rug was a much more protracted job. It had been painstakingly assembled from strips cut from old coats that the family had finished with or that mother had managed to buy for 'next to nowt' at a jumble sale; each strip was prodded through a piece of hessian to form a loop. Cutting strips with scissors left a painful lump on a finger. 'Mrs King had a rug-making frame which she loaned out. You had your part of the rug to do and had so much work to finish every night. If you dawdled, you got clouted.'

The rugs made by one West Riding family had a distinctive pattern, featuring the outline of a diamond in the middle, with lighter hues round about and with a border that was all black, all red or both black and red. 'You had a new rug every Christmas; the old one went into the kitchen. After that, if you had a dry cellar it finished up on t'cellar floor. If t'cellar was damp, carpet would go mouldy and smell. Onnyroad, it finished up in t'dustbin.' The pegged rug was given a good shake every Saturday, having absorbed so much muck that when it was carried back into the house it seemed only half the previous weight. A craze developed for coconut matting, which had to be taken outdoors and beaten several times a week.

Heat from the fire rose to the creel, a rack that might be raised or lowered using rope and pulleys. It was here that the family clothes were dried or aired. Sometimes, oatcakes might be seen dangling from the creel, looking for all the world like stiff wash-leathers.

A mill town family was also equipped with a clothes horse or 'winter hedge', a wooden frame in two pieces, bound together so that they could be opened to form a V shape for stability, and used to hang not-quite-dry washing on. Great attention was paid to the 'airing' of clothes. 'My mother always aired mine properly – from my liberty bodice to my shirt.' Apart from those bought at Whitsuntide, clothes were handed down in the large families that were customary at the time. 'You didn't wear them out because you were growing so quickly.'

Dick Gregson, a native of Brighouse, told me that he had formed a great love and admiration for his stepmother through watching her cope with what appeared to be impossible circumstances. She was, in Dick's words, a little mouse-like woman. His father introduced her to the family with the words: 'This is your new mother!' Father then left the house. The pubs had opened. 'The poor woman was left to get to know four strange children and to organise a household that had degenerated to near slum conditions.' She started first thing that Monday morning, when – said Dick – 'she gave the girls a "prison crop" and a good dose of anti-vermin ointment! Next thing she mended the sewing machine and started to patch already patched sheets . . . Slowly, painfully, she began to pull us out of the muck.'

A small house and a large family offered little privacy for the parents, especially as the youngest children might be sleeping in the same room. This could be frustrating for the husband; it was rarely so for the wife. Many of the married women of the mill towns appear, from what they have said, to have tolerated sex without finding enjoyment in it. The main reason for this was a fear of conception and the appearance of yet another baby in a household where there was scarcely enough money to clothe and feed the existing children. All too often, the solution for an unwanted pregnancy lay in a visit to a back-street abortionist, who charged £5. 'She just washed you out with soapy water.'

Talk about sex was considered rude. Mothers might be too embarrassed to speak about it to their daughters. There was no sex education at school, and contraception was unknown to most women. It was not unusual for a mill town girl who was expecting a child to be unaware of the part of her anatomy from which it would appear. One woman who had had an exceptionally bad time awoke and saw the baby, and promptly asked the nurse for details of how it had come into the world. Big families were common.

There were five of us, apart from mum and dad. We

all lived quite happily in a little terraced house. There couldn't have been much room. A girl I played with was one of fourteen children. When I got a bit older, and went out with another girl, I found she was one of a family of sixteen. There were so many, her mum had to bake on a Sunday to keep 'em all fed. It was considered shocking to do something like baking on a Sunday.

One couple had twenty-one children. 'At meal-times, they all sat on forms around a big table. He was a big fat man; she was a right thin little woman. She died young. Too many kids!'

The kind of care a child could be given depended on the family finances. When a new mother could not afford to buy a cot, she kept the baby in a drawer. Her husband made 'a sort of cart' to hold the drawer, and thus they had a pram! Ostermilk and gripe water were fed to the infant whose mother was unable to breast-feed. Ostermilk did not give the child 'a lot o' wind . . . There was also a syrup to get rid of wind and tummy ache; but it tended to clag the bairn up. It wasn't as good as gripe water.'

The mill town housewives elevated cleanliness to the level of godliness. At home, their conscious hours were devoted to keeping dirt at bay. They scrubbed, brushed and scoured their homes until the meanest place became a palace. Before brushing a dusty carpet, it would be bestrewn with damp tea leaves. The high point of all this activity was the ritual of spring cleaning. 'We'd no proper meals. I used to boil a pan o'peas while I were doing summat else. We had fish and chips more than not. It seemed to go on for weeks.' At spring-cleaning time, carpets were taken out into the yard to be draped from a clothes line and attacked with cane beaters to remove the dust.

An East Lancashire housewife was so 'particular' that she did not permit a bit of ash to settle on the floor for more than a minute before 'she was at it with brush and shovel'. Her husband returned home one day to find that she had scrubbed the face of the alarm clock, which was now 'white as an angel'. There was just one thing – the clock no longer worked after its bath!

Washing the flags outside the house was an almost sacred duty:

> I once clouted somebody with a floor-cloth for walking on mi flags before they'd dried. I didn't get job done as soon as the others. I washed all the flags, from the lady's house next door to the end of my house – it was double-fronted – and this ere person came down t'street.
>
> Instead of stepping off into t'road, and going round, she walked on the flags I'd just done. So I made no more to do – I clouted her with my floor-cloth, right across her legs. She played heck wi' me. I said: 'Well, you shouldn't have walked on mi wet flags. I can't stop anybody walking on 'em when they're dry.'

The front street, being at the final approach to a terminal, was used by buses, so this woman regularly brushed half the road. (And she 'couldn't abide' a squeaky pram and was known, when one approached, to appear at her door with an oil can and say to the startled owner of the pram: 'Let me put a drop of oil on.')

In most terraced houses, the living room was also a kitchen. The dominant feature was a cast-iron fireplace, surmounted by a mantelpiece adorned by a clock and pot dogs or, perhaps, a pot horse. 'At least, it was half a horse – a horse sliced down the middle; the other half stood at the opposite end of the mantelpiece.' On one side of the standard mill town fireplace lay a side boiler, covered with a heavy lid; on the other was an oven.

The drawers of tables, sideboards and wardrobes contained surprising objects, such as packets of candles bought 'in case'. And almost every drawer had at least two bars of soap 'to make the clothes smell nice'. Phil Smith, chatting with an auctioneer at Colne who knew more than anyone about the contents of old people's houses, heard him say: 'I should think that in this area there's been more soap used for making things smell nice than for washing. I'm not saying that the old folk of Colne are mucky but that nearly all of them keep soap in their wardrobes and drawers.'

I recall the summer days when a dominant sound in every house was that of houseflies buzzing against the windows. Long, sticky 'fly-papers' adorned the gas brackets indoors.

Each day had its special tasks. The Monday wash ritual has already been described, with all its possing (stirring the washing in the tub with a special stick), scrubbing, boiling, blueing (dolly blue was also used to treat wasp stings!) and starching, dampening, folding and ironing clothes. Everywhere you could see pieces of carbolic soap and suds. Women wearing old clothes, print pinafores and twisted lisle stockings would reach out to peg clothes on the lines. A Colne man, in jocular vein, remarked: 'Work kept women fit – you should have seen th'arms on 'em. On Monday, they were twining [turning] the mangle for hours. After that, and all the other jobs, women were glad enough to get upstairs to bed and they didn't need rocking before they fell asleep.'

A Yeadon woman recalls when washing took all day. 'The children had to help. Each did so many posses and they also helped to empty wash-tubs and to fold sheets. The mangle had wooden rollers and a big turning wheel made of iron.' In front was a tub. 'A sort of gate was balanced along the top of the tub in two rowlocks; one swung the handle of the gate – we called it a swiller – to and fro to agitate the clothes and water.' It was a much more advanced and refined concept than the old 'dolly' that grandmother knew.

In those days, given good weather, every scrap of washing was dried outdoors. It was fascinating, as I wandered along the back streets of Skipton in the early 1930s, to see the acres of billowing fabric. I once ran the gauntlet of some angry housewives. The bike that I was learning to ride ran out of control through several lines of washing, and ended with the front wheel jammed between a wall and a lamp post. Among the objects on view when the town was 'dressed overall' in honour of the god of hygiene were pillow-cases made from unbleached calico, bought cheaply from the mill; and in some of the meaner parts of mill towns you saw clothes that were almost literally rags. 'I can remember boys coming to school in bare feet and jumpers that were just holes, surrounded by frayed wool.'

The pawnbroker was visited by those who were living up to their means; it was not unusual for a suit to be taken in on Monday morning, only to be redeemed on Friday. It was then available for another week-end. Some of the items on the clothes lines had been bought at bargain prices because they had been 'popped' but not redeemed.

One old Brighouse lady told me:

When I came home from school on a Monday, I always had socks to wash. My sister had done the rest of the washing. She left the socks for me. I had every one to wash by hand. I rubbed them up and down the board. On Tuesday night, when they were dry, I had to darn 'em.

I was in the Guides at that time; and the Guides started at 6.30. So between coming home from school, till half past six, I had to have my tea, help to wash up and darn as many socks as I could. If I didn't quite manage it, I'd stick some behind t'cushion on t'sofa while I came back again.

My brother was a shocker with socks. In those days, lads wore knickerbockers, wi' long stockings, and he always went through t'knee of a stocking. I'd that great hole to mend. Many a time, it was so big I had to do it in three stages. Before today, I've put a whole ball of wool in a hole. Then, of course, he always stuck his big toe through.

7   Food and Drink

They used to laugh about all the fish and chip shops we had in Lancashire, but it was a handy meal for anybody who'd been working all th'day and didn't want to bother wi' cooking.

A former weaver at Colne

I used to go shopping at eight o'clock on a Saturday night. I could get a rabbit and a quarter of a stone of potatoes, one pound of onions and a pound of carrots for a shilling.

A Brighouse woman, born in 1906

In the mill towns, from Bolton to Bingley and from Darwen to Dewsbury, fish and chips from a 'chip shop' provided a quick hot meal costing just a few coppers. This appealed to those married women who worked in the mills.

Myra Marsh, who has researched shopping customs at Denton near Manchester, mentions the custom of leaving a 'basin' at the shop early in the day, into which the fish and chips would later be put. The ritual enabled a customer to collect the order without the necessity of queuing at a busy time. The shape of the receptacle was immaterial; it was always called a 'basin'.

Another advantage of fish and chips was that the ratio of fish to chips need not be constant. In affluent times, a portion of fish per person might be purchased. Yet it was possible to divide the fish between three or four, using the cheaper chips to make up the rest of the meal. In some families, indeed, fish was never bought for the children.

My own youthful appetite for fish and chips was always sharpened by the protracted queuing, during which patience was a necessity and not just a virtue. At mealtimes, queues often extended from the shop on to the pavement. The normally silent queue shuffled forward, a few steps at a time, as fry-up succeeded fry-up. A sizzling sound indicated that more fish or another load of chipped potatoes had been placed in the pans.

Grunting and growling might be heard if someone jumped the queue by joining a friend or, in a loud whisper, requested that someone near the front might get some additional fish and chips for them. The youngest children, standing on tiptoe so that they might see above the counter, would wait until the staff had their backs to the customers and then quickly suck vinegar from the bottle. And every child would wistfully request 'some scraps, mister'.

It was pleasurable to run home with the fish and chips in their crinkly brown wrapping-paper resting beneath my jumper, 'to keep them warm'. They in turn kept me warm on chilly evenings. The under-the-jumper treatment did strange things to the shape of the fish, giving them a fluke-like flatness!

Each shop was known for the quality, or otherwise, of its products. At one, t'batter's like armour-plating. Another was stingy with chips. Most shops, in that highly competitive age, provided first-class service and high-quality food, though the modern stomach would turn at the sight of a hunk of dripping floating in the pan like an off-white iceberg. One of the Skipton fish and chip shops stood beside Mill Bridge, which spans the Springs Canal.

So popular was this shop, and so eager were many of its customers to eat the food in the open air, that the canal became littered with discarded paper, to which small chips and oddments of fish still adhered. Anyone walking along the towpath on Sunday detected a strong tang of vinegar.

Alfred Wainwright, reared in back streets and poverty at Blackburn, became a household name through his unique walking guides to the Lake District fell country. A.W. was but one of many Lancastrians who escaped from the long shadows of a mill town to find a sort of heaven lying to the north. His first viewing of Lakeland occurred when he was 23; he died early in 1991, aged 84, having spent every minute he could with the wind on his face and a vista of mountains before him. A Wainwright guide book was written and illustrated by hand, being printed directly from the pages he produced. He did not entirely forget his native area. Twice a week he broke off from his evening stint of fine penmanship to follow the fortunes of the characters in 'Coronation Street'. And several times a week, he sampled fish and chips.

When he lived by himself at Kendal, his weekly order of food from the grocer's – an order which did not vary in the slightest from one week to the next – was supplemented by fish and chips. If his printer wished to give him a special treat, he took him to a chip shop. When he was interviewed by Sue Lawley for the radio programme 'Desert Island Discs' and was asked what he would like to see on his island, he anxiously inquired: 'Will there be a chip shop?' One featured in his television series 'Coast to Coast' – in this case the shop at Kirkby Stephen, which is roughly halfway between St Bees and Robin Hood's Bay. A.W., a connoisseur of fish and chips, preferred to eat them from the paper, as he had done during those early years in Blackburn. And the mill town passion for the deep-fried meal-in-one endures into an age when people are becoming finicky about their food.

During the week, only the children had breakfast at home. Much was made of high tea – for the workers, returning home shortly after 5.30, expected a substantial repast. After all, 'it's thee stomach 'at 'ods thee back up!'

It was a time of relatively cheap food. At Cleckheaton (and doubtless elsewhere) it was possible to buy 'old milk', by which was meant 'blue milk' – what was left after the cream had been separated off for the making of butter and cheese. 'Mother used it for baking bread.' A Huddersfield child of before the 1914–18 war recalled in adulthood how he had accompanied his mother when she was shopping on a Friday evening. His job was to carry the flour. 'For some unknown reason, the flour was always carried in a poke, a sort of cloth bag. I usually stuck it on my head!'

On baking day, the fireplace came into its own. The housewife was adept at making a hot fire and then shifting the coals around so that they were well positioned to both heat water in the boiler and raise the oven to the right temperature for the baking in hand. And every self-respecting housewife made her own bread. 'She was a great baker, was mother. She also baked brown teacakes, currant teacakes, plain teacakes and seed teacakes. She made lovely sponge-cakes, currant loaves and seed loaves. It was all simple, good stuff. It did no harm to your stomach.'

At Brighouse, 'I baked a stone of flour. A quarter of it went into currant teacakes and the rest into bread. I always had a right big jam, apple or mincemeat pasty. If visitors were expected at the week-end, I'd make a big cake.' Other items mentioned to me by West Riding housewives were fruit loaves and fruit-cakes, and flat or 'fatty' cakes. Delicacies included potted meat, suet and dumplings.

In both Yorkshire and Lancashire, a meat and potato pie was a staple food in many working-class homes. The meat was usually beef. Corner shops had pies for sale to textile operatives at dinner-time. A Brighouse woman describes such a pie as being prepared in a dish with a crust, 'which had a little hole in the middle. I never used a "pie-holder" to hold t'crust out of t'gravy. My crusts never flopped in. There was too much good stuff underneath!' In Bradford a steaming pie was the centrepiece of the main window at the Niagara in Ivegate and Robert's in Kirkgate. Pre-1914, a good helping of pie cost fourpence!

The Lancashire hot-pot was traditionally made with mutton chops, or bones and scraps left over from the Sunday meat dish, covered with thin, sliced potatoes. It was under no circumstances 'mash'. The sliced potatoes remained flat and distinctive. Other vegetables, such as peas, lentils and sliced carrots, might be added. One West Riding man, who did not seem to think much of the food of yesterday, recalled with a shiver a meat dish served up in his family. It contained 'some monstrous offal-type meat' or 'awf a pund o' t'worst end o' t'neck.'

Housewives were capable of making something special in quick time, but some dishes needed much attention. It is related that once when a special guest arrived at a West Riding house, the mid-day meal was still being prepared, so mother asked her son to take the visitor into the front room while she finished the cooking. The boy and the visitor got on so well that the young lad confided: 'I know what we're going to have for pudding today!' The visitor inquired what was in store. 'Jam roly-poly pudding,' said the boy, adding: 'Mum's only got one stocking on today.'

A housewife performed wonders with a parcel of meat and bones from the butcher's shop. 'My mother put them in a large earthenware stewpot in the fire oven. It gently stewed all afternoon. My father had a large helping when he came home from the mill: he ate the stew with chunks of home-made bread. The coalman called about 8 p.m. for his money and, of course, he had to have a plateful.'

Of home-prepared food, in a working-class home, the mid-day meal on Sunday was the week's culinary high spot, the first course being Yorkshire pudding with good rich gravy – not 'weshin'-ip watter'. This was succeeded by the meat course, then something-with-custard, depending on the state of the family economy. Always it was Bird's custard. At least the design on the packet was cheerful. Many a family partook of rice pudding, 'wi' a sprinkling o' nutmeg on'.

If mutton featured on the menu, then the mill town mother's last task before meal-time was to nip a few sprigs of mint from the clump growing in a bucket of soil near the kitchen door. Quickly she would shred the leaves, holding the knife by the handle against the board, and working the blade rapidly up and down, slicing finely. The mint was then stirred up in vinegar, with a dash of sugar, as almost-instant mint sauce.

For a poor family, the Sunday repast would feature stewing steak. For the very poor, at other times it would be bread and butter, with perhaps a little ham. One weaver's daughter, in the household where mother was the only wage-earner, recalled: 'Many a time, if it was getting near pay day and mother had only one warp in, there'd be a slice of bread each for us – nothing for her. I remember her cutting a single piece of bread and handing out the pieces with the words: "Go to your auntie, and ask her to put some margarine on it."' The street where this family lived had few scavenging birds and, I was told, it boasted the leanest sparrows in England. Recalling when the pantry was quite literally bare, the weaver's daughter said that the family was saved by a representative of the Labour Party, who brought along some flour, barm (yeast), jam, margarine and tea. 'Mother set to. She soon had the oven going. She baked some bread. It was lovely to smell – and lovely to eat.'

Theoretically, children could not starve. In the leanest times, charitable folk distributed food, or there were soup kitchens and – as a sort of safety net – the Education Authority provided tickets that might be exchanged for

A loom at Queen Street Mill

Joan Collins, of Briercliffe,
one of the weavers of
Queen Street Mill.
She is holding a shuttle.

Weaving shed at Pecket Well

A clogger at Hebden Bridge

Woollen mills in
the Huddersfield district

A back street in Colne

Tramcar and motor car at Utley, Keighley, in 1934

The knocker-up
in a Lancashire
mill town

Workers in a Dewsbury blanket mill

Women at work in a spinning mill

'Pulling back' on detecting a fault in a weaving shed

Lancashire weavers. The young woman wears an apron known as a 'brat'

Many people went to pick over the nearest slag heap for coal, like this one near Dewsbury in 1926

The coalman's horse and cart

Burnley day trippers outside York Minster

Off to the coast by charabanc

food. Two lads attending a Burnley school were so thin they were given free meals. An old friend of mine who was at that school relates:

At a minute to noon, every day, they turned out, went to the headmaster's desk, received a ticket each, and walked a mile and a half down into the town, in summer heat or winter snow, without coats. They went to a wooden hut where one or two women stood over two cauldrons in which stew was cooked. Each of the lads, standing in the open, received a bowl of stew and a chunk of bread.

The housewife strove to feature, at the Sunday mid-day meal, a good joint of meat. She knew that the best time to get one cheaply was on the previous evening, just before the butchers closed their shops or market stalls, for there were no refrigerators, and any meat remaining unsold was disposed of cheaply. A Brighouse man recalls:

Men floated round the pubs, then back to the market, trying to get a joint at a low price. The prices of meat fell as the evening wore on. Drunken men were seen clutching pieces of meat as they reeled around the town, going into pubs. By the time the meat arrived at their homes, it was a pretty mangled mess, but it was good meat.

And a woman living in the same period relates:

I got a leg of veal that had a big knuckle. Still, there was plenty o' meat on it. That veal lasted a day or two. The last little bits were made into hash [a thick stew with potatoes] on Tuesday. A trip to the market late on Saturday evening might also result in some cheap fish. At Colne, in the late 1920s, a fishmonger, wishing to clear his stock before closing for the week-end, shouted: 'Any fish you like for a tanner.'

Sunday was also memorable if there was 'comp'ny for tea' and mother took a tin of salmon, also a tin of pears, from the pantry. The salmon was augmented by bread crumbs, plus a little butter to 'bind' it, and used for sandwiches. At Brighouse,

We had jelly and custard on Sunday teatime. Mum insisted that each of us had a slice o' bread with it. I hated having the jelly, custard and bread in my mouth at the same time. When I think about it, I should have eaten the bread first. You didn't think about such things in those days; you just did what you were told!

Tuesdays and Fridays were 'fish days'. A fishmonger who toured parts of Burnley with his fish on a flat cart sold plaice to the better-off families and, in the case of those with limited means, an ugly-looking fish called a 'gurnard'. It was notable for the incredible number of bones that supported the flesh. Mothers were continually warning their children to chew the fish well to detect bones. If, during the meal, someone spluttered when a bone stuck in his throat, a piece of dry bread was gulped down. As one of the parents would say: 'If yon bone won't come up, then it mun go down!'

In November, bonfires flared from any handy patches of waste ground, and mother made some claggy 'bonfire toffee', using black treacle. Months later, when springtime came to the mill towns, allotments were cultivated, not just as a hobby but to supplement the larder. It was all part of the mill town survival game in straitened times. Rhubarb and custard, being ultra-cheap, were served at many a meal. How the average gardener kept his temper, when gangs of boys wandered across his plot, I will never know. The bamboo canes he purchased were often purloined for games featuring Robin Hood and the Green-wood. Delicacies like raspberries and strawberries were never allowed to ripen. What escaped the boys fell to the blackbirds.

Meanwhile, week after week, children watched the old miracle of loaves rising in their tins. They saw mother replenishing the stock of scones, cakes and buns that were kept in airtight tins in the pantry. As well as teacakes, scones and Sally Lunns, puddings and pies, traditional foods included parkin, treacle tart and cheesecake, oven-bottom cake, pickles – and jam, lots of jam. For children, there were spoons to be licked and basins to be cleaned out!

Special events included the Faith Tea at Chapel, which was a rib-bender: so much food was assembled, it took the average person a few days to return to a normal shape. A Faith Tea was one in which each person brought some food – half a dozen tarts or a cake, some sandwiches or a fruit loaf. One man once shocked a chapel assembly by proclaiming: 'I've more faith than t'lot on you; I've browt nowt.' At that Chapel, they began to use the alternative name for the meal, which is Jacob's Join. The Chapel was also good at organising pie and pea suppers, both pies and peas being easy to warm up. After some special service or a concert, the room would be cleared, trestle tables arranged and overspread with snow-white linen, and the meal would be set out. Grace was always said (or sung) before such a meal. It was heart-warming to hear a hundred lusty voices rendering: 'Praise God from whom all blessings flow . . . '

Lancashire was noted for its meat products and its cakes. The names of some cakes are famous the world over. Eccles cakes were at first sold at fairs or wakes. Bury was famous for its simnel cake. Chorley cake was a delicacy. The mill towns favoured 'savoury ducks', haslet, brawn, potted meat, cow heel, and pigs' heads or trotters.

Pigs' trotters and Bolton have long been interconnected, the local football team being known as 'Trotters'. The food consists of the edible parts of a pig's foot, boiled at the tripe works (the cleaves having been removed). The finished product resembles a mass of transparent jelly; it is eaten with salt.

Some towns had their pay (pea) 'oiles, known primly as hot pea saloons, about which more will be written later. A patron would be confronted by two or three cauldrons, in which were to be seen various types of pea, which were sold in small white basins, to be consumed on the premises. Salt and vinegar were available. A helping of peas cost a halfpenny; one ate the peas and drank off the liquid. You might have a plate of peas for a penny. Or, for fourpence, a ham sandwich made with a teacake. It is recalled that the helping of ham was so generous, it hung out all round the edges of the teacake. The coffee taverns sold steam pie, or meat and potato pie, offered with or without gravy. A piece of Yorkshire pudding cost a penny.

There were seasonal dishes. Shrove Monday was associated with shallow-fried potato scollops. Shrove Tuesday was the day for pancakes. On Ash Wednesday, the main meal was that thick stew with potatoes known as 'hash'. Fritters, served on the Thursday, were made with a pastry-like dough mixed with apples, then shaped into rounds about three inches in diameter and an inch thick. In Calderdale, at Eastertime, dock pudding is made with *Polygonum bistorta*, a plant that thrives locally.

Farmers and small-holders provided fresh country produce for their friends at relatively low prices. The manager of a mill at Morton, near Keighley, told me: 'In the late 1920s and early 30s, I bought from the overlooker, who kept hens, scores of dozens of eggs at 10d per dozen, and scores of dressed boiling fowls at 2s 6d each.' Pig products became more easily available to large numbers of people with industrialisation and a rising urban population. On most days, at Skipton, I passed near 'Porky' Holmes's shop, which had a representation of a pig on the gable end. 'We specialise in the Pig and its Products,' said the sign, in gigantic letters.

Black puddings were universally enjoyed. When a pig was slain, its blood was collected in a bucket and stirred until it coagulated and darkened. To it were added groats and pieces of fat about the size of dice. Herbs gave added flavouring. The skins for the pudding were made from pigs' intestines. Tripe was cheap and nourishing. Easily digested, it was reputed to 'clean the stomach'. 'Elder', from the udder of a cow, was sliced thin and traditionally eaten with salt, vinegar, pepper, brown bread and butter.

Pride in belonging was everywhere evident. Many years ago, when chatting with traders in the Halifax covered market, I heard Bradford described as 'a cow town'. The man added, proudly, that 'Halifax is a heifer and bullock town'. And I once asked a Dewsbury man if local people had a special fondness for savoury food. I was thinking of a contest between savoury and sweet, but he replied, laconically: 'Aye – if they could afford it!'

If all else failed, and there were still a few pennies in the kitty, there was always the chip shop . . .

8 Life in the Street

There was life before 'Coronation Street'. But it didn't amount to much.

Russell Harty, a native of Blackburn

When I came to Nelson, over 70 years ago, they hadn't even made t'street up. Those houses look as good today as they did then.

An owner-occupier

The street was an entity. It formed part of the tight parochial structure of the mill town. The street was a cosy place, packed with people, and always with something going on. In this it reflected the physical overcrowding of the weaving shed, for the mill-towner is nothing if not gregarious. 'Nobody thought about locking their doors,' recalls a Keighlian. 'Folk went in and out of houses all day long. At times, at my Grannie's, we had to take it in turns to breathe. It's different today. You never know who's about. You'd be daft not to lock up behind you.'

The street does survive, in a fashion, though children who are not watching television must now play around the many parked cars. The street is less clean than it used to be, when flagstones were scrubbed weekly and some people even swept the roadway itself.

Every sort of drama might be observed in the street.

With the houses cheek-by-jowl, no secrets could be hidden from the neighbours. Now virtually everything takes place behind closed doors. I used to see noisy confrontations between neighbours – rows over clothes lines or alleged damage caused by a child. I once saw a woman advance on her neighbour with a carving knife, only to pass by and cut down a clothes line. It was a small matter of territory – a trival matter transformed by temper into something big. The case went to Court, where, under the amused smiles of the magistrates, the quarrel was resolved and the defendant's fine was paid by the aggrieved party!

Squabbling was a periodic feature of street life. When two women with rasping tongues confronted each other, even the cats and dogs fled. Antagonism might take the form of 'not talking'. Someone would say, with pride, that they were 'not talking' to particular women. The quarrels of yesteryear were recalled. Everyone seemed to have a story about the next-door neighbour cutting his throat in the yard.

Everyone knew his or her neighbour's business. Ears were cocked for titbits of information that might become gossip, such as the fact that Joyce's husband had 'run away' with one of the mill girls. Housewives who tolerated their husband's excessive drinking, and who overlooked his lack of interest in the condition of the house, would not tolerate infidelity. Divorces were extremely rare. The divorce section of our local newspaper hardly ever ran to more than a dozen lines, in small type, tucked away at the bottom of a page, and each case was something to be tut-tutted over by the other women. Now and again a father might leave home. He always moved quickly. As a small boy I wondered why it was that couples 'ran away' with each other. Why did they not choose their moment – and walk!

Another serious crime against the morality of working-class family life was to be physically fit but disinclined to find a job. Layabouts were despised. The work ethic ruled almost everyone's daily life. The wife of an idle man, returning home, hoped to hear her husband say that he had found work, for he was to have spent the day looking for it. 'I haven't managed owt,' he would say, 'but I've getten thee a bit more washing to tek in.'

When the summer sun was aglow, and the children were on holiday from school, there was a constant party spirit in the street. House doors were left wide open all day long. Children ran in and out of the houses as they wished. Or they 'ran' errands; *they* never walked! The person who asked a child to 'run' usually handed over a copper or two, which the child dutifully gave to mother 'for the gas'. In the 1920s, a penny was also the price of an egg. Children were both seen and heard. Clogs thumped on the flagstones. Two boys, having a minor dispute, would brace themselves for a possible fight, not with fists but with clogs. They would let fly with their feet. 'Look out,' one boy would say, 'or you'll feel my carkers [irons].' The parents, taking a break from work, would gossip in the sunshine. Little girls played house with clothes-horses overspread with old sheets. Grandparents raked back through the years and roused the memories of what they considered to be happier times.

The street had its informal, voluntary social service long before this became a council department. If an old lady needed to summon help from next door, she would knock on the fireback with a poker. When a Barnoldswick woman lost her wage packet, and sobbed, friends and neighbours had a whip-round and raised about £3 to 'put her on' for another week. (Sometime later, the woman found her wage packet in a carrier bag. She offered to pay back the money, but everyone told her to keep it.)

A few women chatted as they washed the windows with their long brushes. On Fridays, after doing the housework, they donned clean aprons as they waited for their husbands to arrive home with their wages. The local pub was a temptation on pay day. It was up to the wife to ensure that her 'hubby' did not sneak by the house to the pub and drink his money away. Not that she wasn't prepared to give him a bob or two so that he could go to the pub or club. Having done this, she knew where he was and what he was doing! He might ask for a 'breaking in' – a few coppers to get into a pub. There was always a chance he would meet somebody who'd be silly enough to pay for a pint for him!

In Skipton, which was hardly a den of vice, I once saw a drunken man returning home. He rapped on the door, leaned against it, and when it was opened by his wife he fell – stiff as a plank – into the living room. Another covered the last few yards of the back street through a barrage of old wine bottles hurled at him by an irate woman and her support team: the children, who ran up and down the cellar steps for more bottles, which were lined up on a wall waiting to be hurled at the miscreant.

At Brighouse, 'Zingo Nick's' – a lodging house on Commercial Street – was a place to pass at top speed, especially on Saturday nights. 'The lodgers were always drunk. Some of 'em would be fighting.' At another lodging place, on Bradford Road, you could look down from the street into the cellar and see the men scrubbing shirts:

> Each man had only one working shirt, and there he was, stripped to t'waist, scrubbing away so it would be clean for Monday morning. And didn't those men swear at you if you stood and watched them. But I wasn't flayed [afraid] of them. I was on t'street and they were in t'cellar! If they offered to come round t'corner – I shot off!

Some streets were part of busy urban thoroughfares. 'Every morning, a man with a big Airedale dog came down our street. He carried a pudding basin in a red handkerchief, which he would heat up on the steam pipes at the mill.' This man was the gatekeeper of Turner's Mill, Brighouse, a building which went up in smoke in 1973. 'It was a huge fire. My dad was a fireman and my mum made cocoa for the firemen, so we knew all about it.'

In some terraces, where most of the children had grown up and married, the usual rowdy atmosphere was absent. An air of gentility had replaced it. A woman who spent childhood holidays with relatives near Rochdale in the early 1930s recalled the well-ordered routines of the housewives. In the average home, she said, there were two classes of carpet – a good carpet for use during the week-end and an older one which served during the week. 'On a Monday morning, the best carpet was rolled up and put under the sideboard. There it would remain 'till week-end. My auntie used to put old stockings on the legs of the best table to stop it getting knocked about.' On the bus journey through Lancashire to auntie's house near Rochdale, this child was fascinated by the 'leaded lights' in windows.

I used to notice how many of them had 'lights' and the type of pattern used. It varied a lot. Many a house had a vase of artificial flowers in the main window. If my mother couldn't have got real flowers, she wouldn't have bothered. But it was the windows that attracted my attention. I suppose you had 'arrived' when you could afford to have 'leaded lights'.

At this terrace near Rochdale where the child used to stay, the neighbours were well disposed to each other, 'always in and out of each other's homes'. In the evening, a small group of women would don their mill brats (aprons) and sit crocheting and talking about the mill. Their husbands had gone off to the working men's club. 'To me, a little gathering of women seemed so homely I've never forgotten it. They crocheted "duchess" sets and antimacassars. Whichever house you went into, you'd see the same pattern.' The women spoke distinctly. Many had worked in the mill. 'You could tell they were used to speaking against noise. They opened their mouths a lot. They made themselves heard without shouting. I suppose they were used to lip-reading.'

The mill town street and its environments were, to children, an area of mystery and excitement. In summer, the children were called in for bed when it was still warm and sunny. In winter, they played out 'till it's dark'. The street pastimes included hop-scotch on the stone flags, skipping under the street lamps, whipping tops, and running with hoops. 'The boys had bully-bools [hoops with a metal rod attached by a hooked end] and the girls had wooden hoops which they hit with a stick.' As winter relaxed its hold and the days lengthened, small groups of boys played taws (marbles). Some of the taws were glass balls taken from the necks of lemonade bottles. The girls played with shuttlecock and battledore. 'We had a game where you had to creep up on the one standing at the front without them hearing. If they heard you, they spun round and pointed. Then you had to go to the back again.'

Skipping was a diversion for the girls; as they skipped they chanted one or two of the refrains that had been passed down through the generations:

> The wind, the wind, the wind blows high,
> The rain comes scattering from the sky;
> She is handsome, she is pretty,
> She is a girl of London city.

> Touch the floor,
> Reach for the sky;
> Throw your arms out wide
> And call so-and-so in . . .

'When they went out, you went in.' In my native West Riding, small girls skipped and chanted:

Raspberry, strawberry, gooseberry jam;
Tell me the name of your young man . . .

Children also sang 'Green grow the leaves on the oak
tree'. Were they perpetuating the spirit of pre-industrial
Lancashire?

They played their own version of 'knur and spell',
which was called 'buck and stick'. The stick might be an
old picking-stick from the mill. Made of ash, it was very
strong. You tipped the buck, which flew into the air; you
struck it hard, and then you ran. Then there was 'relievo',
which featured a tin can, a convenient manhole cover on
which to place it, and a knowledge of all the best hiding
places. For football, rolled-up rags served as the ball. An
old tennis ball might be used for cricket. Wickets were
chalked on the wall of the nearest friendly native. The lad
who owned the bat and ball naturally appointed himself
as cricket captain. Should his authority be challenged, he
went home sulking – taking the equipment with him!

There were crazes, such as diabolo. The game consisted
of two sticks joined by a cord. One had to spin and
balance on the cord a top-like bobbin. Some exponents
spun the bobbin and then threw it in the air, catching it
again as it descended. Truth-or-dare, tin-can squat, hide-
and-seek, leapfrog – these were played in terraces dwarf-
ed by the mills and their chimneys. At one West Riding
town, 'we used to tie a parcel on a string and hop over
the wall. When a passer-by leaned down to pick the parcel
up, we yanked on the string. We used to tie a penny
t'same way.'

In spring, when the dandelions that had sprung from
every crack on the ground put on their bright yellow caps,
and the curlews had flown over the mill towns on their
way from the wintering grounds by the sea to their moorland nesting haunts, small girls might produce, of all
things, a maypole.

A Burnley man recalls: 'It was a broom handle with

two wooden hoops fixed on the top. The hoops were interlaced, decorated with specially frilled paper of various colours. A bell hung from the hoops, and at the top was the semblance of a crown. Ribbons extended from the top of the broomstick.' A small group of girls, usually five, would tour their part of town with the maypole. It was set down at street corners, and the girl who supported the pole sat on a small stool. The others, dressed in special clothes made of paper, in pastel shades, had small crowns on their heads. 'They danced to a traditional song, "Round and round the maypole, merrily we go; ippy, chippy, churry, singing as we go!" The chorus was "Hurrah, hurrah, hurrah May Queen". They had a collecting box, of course.'

The old 'uns in the street recalled that in the summers before the 1914–18 war, German bands were popular. The bandsmen wore splendid uniforms with peaked caps, and 'they played the usual German music, marches and waltzes'. At about the same period, a man of vaguely East European origin used to appear in Burnley with a small hand-operated organ on a stick. He had a monkey, which wore a jacket and red fez cap. Once, when the monkey was at work, holding out one hand to passers-by for money, someone noticed it suddenly dart up the fallpipe of a house and cross to a window ledge, to collect a coin from a woman who had appeared at an upstairs window. The monkey returned to ground and slipped the coin in the owner's tin!

Who did not feel their spirits lift when the Salvation Army band arrived to play, to speak, to collect for the funds? A Huddersfield man recalled for me the days of sixty years ago, when 'we kids used to stand in the front row as the Salvation Army band played on Sunday afternoon'. It is said of one small West Riding town that a spinster there, in the 1930s, gave 10s to the Salvation Army collector, who, overcome with joy, said: 'Eh, missis, for that you can have any hymn you like.' She said: 'I'll have 'im wi' t'big drum.' At other times, women Salvationists went round the pubs, with copies of the *War Cry* and a collection box.

What of the pub at the end of the street – the Rover's Return of Anytown? Before the 1914–18 war, a public house was open from 6 a.m. to 11 p.m. during the week, and from noon to 2 p.m. and 7 to 10 p.m. on Sunday. Once there was a multiplicity of small breweries, offering many subtle variations on the theme of 'strong drink'. Take-overs were to greatly limit the choice of drinks. In the High Street at Great Horton (Bradford), prior to 1914, a toper had a choice of twelve pubs and three clubs (Liberal, Conservative and Working Men's) within about a mile. This density of drinking places was fairly typical of the Bradford suburbs.

Every encouragement was given to the public to drink – and drink again. Before 1914, a favoured drinker received a clay pipe, free of charge. I was told of pipes being delivered to a public house or hotel in a sawdust-filled barrel. A dozen or so of the long 'churchwarden' pipes were to be found in the middle, and ordinary pipes were packed round the edges. Black twist was popular, being cut up and then rammed into the bowl of the pipe. The resultant tang and smoke were comparable with standing near an engine shed at a mill.

Beer was delivered in the cask, on drays. The casks were lowered into the cellars of a pub by rope and tackle. It was simpler to get drunk in the old days; the ale was much stronger than it is now. When a man went 'on the rant', he scarcely left his chosen pub for days on end, drinking steadily. Drunken brawls were a feature of town centres on Saturday nights. In Bradford, a Catholic priest nicknamed 'Father Blessing' went on the rounds, restraining any men who had drunk too much and felt pugilistic. One well known publican at Bradford, Albert Cowling, was once so annoyed at the sad state of the approach road to his home that he took advertising space in the *Telegraph and Argus* to harass local authority. One advertisement read: 'See Naples and die. See the state of Birch Lane and be ashamed of your own city.' Some streets were rough indeed.

Street traders were commonplace, as I mentioned in chapter 2. These also included the yeast man, who fared well in days when housewives baked their own bread. Among the denizens of Skipton's streets was a travelling fishmonger, who later rose to the dizzy social heights of Conservative agent. When the ice-cream man rang a handbell, children promptly appeared from their homes and dashed with their enamel mugs for 'a penn'orth, please, mister'. Into each partly filled mug went a wafer. In winter, men who dispensed ice-cream returned to their old haunts to sell roasted chestnuts.

Few people stirred in the winter streets. Bedtime came early but at Nelson, young Stanley Jeeves and his brother, having had baths and a change of pyjamas, would sit up in bed waiting for a weekly treat – the appearance of the pie and hot-pea man, who would arrive swinging a bell and inviting custom for his mushy peas, the container for which fitted a small handcart, with a brazier keeping the food warm. Stanley told me: 'My brother and I could either have a cream horn from the confectioner or a hot pie. Father stood at the door and invited the hot-pea man to enter the house. The pies he bought were then brought up to the bedroom. We ate them while sitting up in bed!'

The knife sharpener (with his machine) was a hardy annual. The last time our cutlery was sharpened, I followed the 'grinder', expecting to see a machine, and stood enthralled as he sharpened the knives on a gable end. Then there were the dustmen, who emptied the middens. And the coalman, with his four-wheeled cart laden with bags of coal, was a regular visitor. His horse left a copious amount of dung that was highly prized by gardeners with roses. Within minutes of a horse defecating, the dung had been transferred to the local rose bushes.

Mercifully, children were not conscious of poverty. A Keighley man recalls that 'we got a slice of jam or some dripping and bread – and away we would go to enjoy ourselves in our own way, exploring the alleys at the town centre. Sometimes we clambered on the roofs as well. I don't recall a single case of wilful damage or vandalism.'

The street eventually became restrictive, as children got older, and a young person would wander off to where he or she might meet someone of the opposite sex. A place where young folk walked up and down, sizing up possible mates, was known as a 'monkey run'. In due course a couple clicked (fell in love), and then they would take every opportunity to talk to each other. The street lost its appeal, as they began to look for a place of their own.

9 Off to the Shops

You'd no need to go past t'station for owt you wanted. There were shops galore in Brigg-End.

A native of Colne

My husband's best friend worked in a tripe shop. We used to go on a Saturday for two penn'orth o' bits. They were what he'd cut off when he was weighing out tripe. His boss was right niggly. He hadn't to give an inch more tripe than he needed to.

Heard at Brighouse

In some towns, the pay 'oile (the place where hot peas were sold, described in chapter 7) was high on the list of favourite shops, especially with the young. At Brighouse, 'our pay 'oile was by the canal; the shop had a bow window, and you went down two steps into it. The floor was sanded, the tables scrubbed, and on a big range sat two steaming cauldrons, one with brown peas and the other with green peas. On top was a long tray holding sausages in gravy. There was also a wooden tray with muffs (teacakes). You could have a teacake with a sausage in it – a sort of hamburger.'

The owner, Edmund Stake, wore a pinafore and a flat cap. 'We used to go swimming, then call at the smithy to watch him shoeing horses, and then make our way to the pay 'oile. On Friday, we sometimes had our dinner here.

We then took some peas home for the rest of the family in a jug we'd taken with us'. Mr Stake would put in some peas, then sausages, then gravy. 'He covered it with a piece of paper that was folded round the top and fitted round the handle, keeping it all warm. As we took it home, we lifted up one side and drank the gravy. We thought mother wouldn't know what we'd done. But, of course, she soon found out.'

During the slump years, money was the stuff that other people had. But you needed it to go shopping. One grim day, Ma found she 'hadn't a penny to my name'. Henceforth, she determined there would always be something in the bank. She would not look destitution in the face again. So Ma scrimped and saved until she had a bank account with a modest balance. Whatever might happen to the family, there was always 'Ma's bit o' brass'. In the context of today, the sum of money was laughably small. It was, of course, known only to Ma until her passing, when we had the temerity to look into her Skipton Building Society account. As a member of the family observed: 'Folk spend more on holidays today.'

The precise sum did not matter in the early 1930s. It was enough to know there was something in reserve as the pulse of West Riding life beat ever more faintly and those without work went into a state of semi-hibernation to save on food and boot leather. On our week-end walks, we passed silent mills and smokeless chimneys, careworn adults and unkempt children. At Gorton, in Manchester, where the situation was much worse, the Salvation Army served pea soup and pudding for tuppence.

In the heyday of the market halls, traders with a wide range of goods on offer assembled at these splendid creations that were notable for their ornate ironwork and glass roofs. They provided the convenience of 'single stop' shopping long before the development of the supermarkets. At the beginning of the century, a greengrocer at Bradford would visit the wholesale market at 6 a.m., and keep his premises open until midnight. In pre-1914 Bradford, many small shops closed at 8 p.m. from Monday to Thursday, at from 9 to 10 p.m. on Friday, and at midnight on Saturday.

Even the corner shop grocer knew his trade through and through in those days when many commodities were delivered in bulk and when the competitive edge might be maintained by variations on a single theme – sugar, for example. The good grocer was skilled at grading sugars; they are not all as sweet as each other. He offered crystal sugar, loaf sugar, cube sugar, granulated, castor and fine sugars, not to mention the brown sugars such as 'Jamaica fines', which looked 'as black as t'fireback'. Teas were graded to suit the local water supply. And many a small-time grocer would grind his own coffee, using a machine with a big black wheel.

Myra Marsh, in her researches into the shopping habits of Denton near Manchester, found that the number of shops there greatly expanded between 1891 and 1915, partly because of the de-skilling process that had taken place in retailing: most stock was now obtained ready-packed from wholesalers or manufacturers. Another factor greatly facilitating the growth of small corner shops was the manufacturers' increasing practice of employing commercial travellers who would visit the shopkeeper, collect his order, arrange dispatch from the warehouse and collect payment later.

Among the trades where packaging had made little progress – most of the stock being bought 'loose' – was green-grocery. A lady recalled that in 1916 her mother would catch the tram to Manchester at 5 a.m. in order to buy her stock of vegetables, fruit and fish at the market. Having no transport of her own, she would return by tram to open up the shop (starting with the remains of yesterday's stock). A man from Hyde near Manchester brought fresh produce from the market on his lorry. He performed this service for many small retailers on the route from Man-

chester to Hyde, having spotted a gap in the chain of
distribution and making a living by filling it. Butchers
with any pretensions to quality would slaughter and dress
their own meat; the small abattoir at the back of the butcher's shop was common until the 1930s.

To a small child, the corner shop was a wondrous place.
Saturday pennies were spent on oranges, on liquorice
roots, sweets or 'hawpenny lucky bags', the contents of
which were once described to me as 'a lot of gluey, gooey,
stringy stuff that you could chew for ever'. Some lucky
bags included a collectable football card. 'Kali' powder
was used to make 'lemonade' or was sucked from a paper
bag through a liquorice tube. I remember the spluttering
effect caused by a sudden rush of sweet dry powder into
the throat. The Saturday penny had excellent purchasing
power, though it might become a halfpenny during lean
years, when a sacrifice was demanded for the good of the
family. My favourite uncle, who habitually jangled coins
in his pocket, usually restored my happiness by remarking: 'Let's see if I've got an odd hawp'ny.' Needless to
say, I was never disappointed.

The corner shop was also a place for cheek to be demon-
strated. A small child might ask: 'Have you any Wild
Woodbines?' When the shopkeeper nodded his or her
head, the child would promptly say: 'Well, tame 'em!' Or:
'Have you any ice buns?' 'Yes.' 'Well – skate on 'em.' Or:
'Two penn'orth o' jelly-round-squares, please.'

One was expected to save out of a penny. A local butcher said to a child who was paying the family bill on behalf
of his mother: 'Here's an 'awp'ny – an' think on: put it in
t'bank!' I was twenty-one years of age before I actually
owned a £5 note.

Once, as I emerged from a shop with a penny lollipop,
which represented almost the top of the price range for
lollipops, a passing Methodist local preacher intoned,
with mock gravity, and in biblical style: 'I see you're
squandering your substance on riotous living.' Bliss was

the state attained by someone who had the means of buying a slab of McGowan's toffee, which had a picture of a Highland cow on the grease-proof wrapper. The toffee was covered by thin, somewhat brittle chocolate which, as the toffee block was bent, fragmented and dispersed like shrapnel. To put a large piece of toffee in the mouth was to induce lockjaw.

The 'house shops' consisted of simple shelves and a counter in what was normally the living room, or a trestle table set up under the window, and all contained cheap sweets, salt, matches, candles, tapers, sewing needles, pins, gravy salt, lemonade and headache powders. The owner of one shop had a constant supply of matches. When a new stock arrived at the shop, she slyly removed one match from each box and put it to one side for her personal use.

The older folk in our communities went to t'Quarp (Co-op). Many doubtless still do. The Co-operative movement as we know it today (and as noted in chapter 3) is said to have begun with the Rochdale 'Pioneers', who rented the ground floor of a building in Toad (t'owd – 'the old') Lane and converted the front room into a store where, with a membership of twenty-eight and a capital of £28, they sold, at first, butter, sugar, flour, oatmeal and candles. There is, however, a claim that an earlier society was founded at Meltham Mills, near Huddersfield. Tradition says that in this small village a group of men clubbed together to buy a sack of flour at sack (wholesale) price. They distributed the flour among themselves at a per-pound price that was still wholesale. The retailer's profit margin was saved and pocketed. This is the principle on which the enormous Co-op movement was to be built.

Some people had a snobbish attitude towards the Co-op. It was of the working class and for the working class. Discipline for employees was strict, wages were poor, but loyalty abounded. To work for the Co-op meant security and a high status. 'I always felt warm, safe and happy at the Co-op,' I was told by a former employee.

Brian Crompton, of Golcar, who grew up amid the busy textile industry in the 1930s in what is still the largest parish in the Colne Valley, tells me that no fewer than six Co-ops were situated within a radius of about one mile from Town End, the centre of Golcar. 'The village is built on a hillside, very much akin to the "Italian style", and therefore the Brook Lane Co-op was in lower Golcar and the two Town End Co-ops in upper Golcar.' It is fascinating to hear of those other Co-ops:

Proceeding from Town End towards Longwood in the Huddersfield direction was the Leymoor Co-op . . . Then 'on t'op at 'thill' – so referred to by older locals – was the hamlet of Scapegoat Hill, where the Co-op boasted the highest 'divi' for miles around. Some Golcar people would even plod up to 'Scapi' in all weathers just to have that extra bonus . . . Lastly, there was the Clough Head Co-op, which was above Golcar also, going in the direction of Slaithwaite.

The Co-op movement offered considerable variety in goods and services, and even in outlook. Mr Crompton again: 'One was the Yellow Co-op and the other the Blue, and as you have already guessed, the Liberals founded the Yellow and the Conservatives the Blue. This caused quite a bit of amusement and sarcasm with Labour people, for after all the Co-op and Labour movements were closely linked.'

Clifford Stephenson, recalling life at Lockwood near Huddersfield before the 1914–18 war, told me he was seven or eight years old when Grannie entrusted him to collect items from the Co-op. To a small boy,

the grocery department, my usual venue, was huge, cavernous, mysterious and rather frightening . . . All

along the right-hand side was a counter for dry goods;
opposite, down the left-hand side, the butter side, lay
another long counter stacked with butter, cheese, lard
and bacon. The hand-operated bacon-slicer – then a
new invention – fascinated me . . . But the butter was
most impressive.

Co-ops were proud of the quality of the 'best butter'
they sold. It was known as Kiel butter, originating I
suppose from the area around the Kiel Canal, which
sends us butter now known as 'Danish'. It came in
kegs, small lightweight tubs that were opened out to
allow the contents to be up-ended on to a large por-
celain plate on the counter – a two-foot-high golden
mass.

The assistants sliced it horizontally by a wire into
four-inch layers, out of which were cut wedges of butter
(like cutting a round cake) of the quantity each customer
required. Often the sides of the lump of butter on the
counter were scored by grooves made by the thumb
nails of customers who gouged out a sample to taste,
perhaps remarking 'It's a bit salty this week, George.'

Mr Stephenson recalls two pipes that came down the wall
behind the counter. Each held treacle. One pipe was for
'dark' treacle (used for parkin and treacle toffee) and the
other was for 'light' treacle. The end of each pipe had a
slide to stop the flow. 'Dexterity and experience were
needed to judge the exact moment at which to cut off the
stream into the container.'

To a lad entrusted with money, and making some Co-
op purchases – sugar, barley, lentils – it was fascinating
to see the goods being scooped up loose from large bags
and then poured into little blue bags. Spice [sweets]
were counted into a cone made of a single piece of
white paper, the bag being twisted at the bottom once
the cone shape had been attained.

Tins of condensed milk were popular with the poor, taking the place of fresh milk in tea and being used by mothers to soothe their babies, the baby's dummy being dipped in the milk.

The son of a Huddersfield woollen spinner, who drew his wage on a Friday, used to be sent on errands to the Co-op with a carpet bag, a flour bag and a £1 note.

The flour bag was more like a pillow-case, being made of some sort of material so that the flour wouldn't come through. After it was filled with flour, I tied it up with a band and then put it into another piece of material and tied it across, both ways. I would carry it on my head. 'The carpet bag, which I held with one hand, was full of things like butter, margarine, sugar, tea, jam, treacle, cigs, tapers, matches, salt, pepper and anything else you can mention. I had a bag full – and some change out of that £1 note. Can you believe it?'

When a transaction at t'Quarp was completed, the manager would demand to know the family number. In my young days, I would say, with due solemnity, 'Two Four Four Nine.' He would write it down, in figures, handing me a check and keeping the carbon copy on file for the records. That check ensured that we would receive our divi (dividend). Repeat the word slowly, with feeling – DIVI. It was a vital part of a poor family's economy. As I mentioned earlier, you could get divi on the dead – if you patronised the Co-op funeral service – and have a 'ham tea' at the Co-op café, as I shall relate.

People rarely forgot their Co-op number. In Manchester, during the lean period of the 1920s and 1930s, the divi ranged from 1s 6d to 2s in the £. A Rusholme woman told me: 'I had an aunt living in Glossop who, through her married life, saved her divi, which at its best was 3s in the £. When she retired, there was quite a nest egg; she put the money towards the purchase of a small herbalist shop at Hadfield.'

At Burnley, 'drawing the divi' just before Wakes Week was a highlight of the year. A woman remarked: 'Mother, now in her eighties, still uses the word 'divi', though in another context – "Let me have a look at my bank account and see how much divi I've getten."' Clifford Stephenson remembers old Mrs Garside

struggling up steep Hanson Lane at Lockwood, humping the traditional carpet bag full of groceries in one hand and a 'flour poke' of two stones of flour in the other. She trailed this all the way from Close Hill, passing Lockwood Co-op on the way – all this for the sake of the bigger 'two and ten' [14p] divi paid by Close Hill Co-op, when Lockwood paid only 'two and eight' [13p].

At Rastrick, near Brighouse, a woman who always shopped at the Co-op told her granddaughter of the days when she could purchase a week's groceries for six children and two adults and still have change from a 10s note. 'She always used her divi to pay her rates.' And a Rochdale lady told me with pride that her grandfather, Joseph Hullows, worked at the Co-op, and that his divi number was low – 242. He was an early member. Her mother shopped at the Co-op and coal was delivered to the house by the Co-op coalman, with his horse and cart. (In Manchester, in the 1920s and 30s, Co-op coal was about £5 a ton.)

At Rishton near Blackburn, between 1921 and 1934, one woman patronised a whole complex of Co-op shops: butcher, grocer, draper, ladies' outfitter, gents' outfitter and tailor, confectioner and – across the side street – the shoe shop and clogger. Such a complex was to be found in most large centres of population.

In the Rishton grocer's shop, which was scented by coffee being ground on the spot, the shelves held Co-op jams and marmalade, tins of golden syrup and black treacle, tinned fruit and tinned salmon. This shop had five counters – three on one side and two on the other. Male assistants had their regular positions behind these counters. 'It was the pre-packed period,' the Rishton woman recalls.

> Sugar and dried goods had to be weighed and put in bags. Butter was weighed out, then patted into shape. Bacon and cheese were cut according to your wishes. Now and again, a rumbling sound in a back room indi-cated that potatoes or bags of flour were slithering down the shutes from a storeroom above. It sounded like thunder when the potatoes came tumbling down.'

The confectioner provided fresh bread, cakes, teacakes, oven-bottom muffins, meat pies and fruit pies, also egg custards. A large assembly room over the shops was used for dances and social events on Friday nights. Co-op premises were at one time a meeting place for old people to discuss their various ailments and grievances.

At the Co-op at Hepworth, near Huddersfield, there was the usual impressive grouping of goods and services – grocery, fruit and vegetables, drapery, butchery and hardware. 'I loved to go upstairs, to where the pots and pans were kept, for they formed a splendid array.' The next room contained bulk supplies of soap, potatoes and flour. 'I can still smell the freshness of "white Windsor" soap. For each pound, you were given a paper wrapper. When you had collected a dozen wrappers, you received a free towel. The cellar was also interesting; it contained large stone slabs where vinegar kegs and barrels of treacle were stored.'

A Bury man recalls a free Co-op library, 'which must have been quite a rarity in 1939'. This man began school in that year, 'when father was called up into the Army. He ran the family errands and remembers Grandma saying: "Tell Gilbert [the Co-op manager] to give you the check so I'll get me divi.'" The toffs were said to go to the Co-op café in the town centre. As I said earlier, the Co-op provided funeral facilities, and also the 'ham teas' which were afterwards much enjoyed by relatives and friends. The story is told of a Co-op funeral at Bury in the 1920s when Grandma and Aunt Martha shared in a funeral repast. On the plates were tongue, ham and beef. It had been raining at the graveside, and Grandma had her umbrella. Before the two ladies left the café, they tipped into the upright umbrella any remaining cold meat from the handiest plates. Grandma used to say that the family lived for a week on those meats! (Grandma decreed in her will that her funeral tea should be held there, and so it was, in the year 1953.)

At Bury, the Co-op had their own Bank. A biscuit factory and a mineral water factory were not far away. A clogger's shop offered footwear of all sizes and types, for men, women and children. From upstairs, in a room where the clogger tapped in the brass nails, came the smell of wood and leather. A child, leaving the clogger with some new or renovated clogs, could not wait to dash them against the pavement so that the 'caulkers' made sparks fly.

When I asked mill town folk for their memories of the Co-ops, I was regaled with information. The Co-op impressed its members by having its own brand names, including 'Wheatsheaf'. Sometimes the Co-op motto, 'Unity is Strength', with a symbol of two hands clasping, was incorporated in the tilework of a shop porch. Gone, but not forgotten, are the 'emporiums'. A lady living at Ashton-under-Lyne recalled one called Arcadia.

Every Saturday, we went to Arcadia for a cup of tea and a toasted teacake. It was the highlight of the week. One met the same people, by and large. Everyone was dressed up. The Co-op was self-sufficient, selling clothes, furniture, hardware, hats, lingerie. In the basement, oil cloth, lino, carpets, rugs, etc. The smell in here was distinctive and lingers in my nostrils yet.

It was the custom at Whitsuntide to buy 'Whit Walk' dress and shoes. She and her mother would visit the hat department, which was 'sheer delight'. This department was on its own, set back from the lingerie section, the walls lined with mirrors, and with deep drawers where the hats were kept wrapped in soft tissue paper. The most fancy hats were on display on old-fashioned wooden hat stands.

Nan would accompany us for *her* Whit hat. She had four hats a year from the Co-op – one for Whit, two for attending Chapel, being bought new in spring and autumn, and a good sensible felt hat for her shopping . . . Also, twice a year, Nan would buy pink corsets with a tortuous array of hooks and eyes and tapes, and combinations in pure soft wool for winter . . . Mum had a new coat every two years.

It was like one big family at the Co-op. 'The manager seemed to spend his time walking about the floor; he wore an immaculate suit and had a red flower in his buttonhole. If he said "Good morning" to you, your day was made!' Both customer and employee adhered to unspoken rules. Everything was old-fashioned. 'I remember dark, heavy wood furnishings and drawers, myriad drawers, full of ribbons, elastic, lace and braid, etc.' A West Riding woman tells of Monday evenings spent learning how the Co-operative Society was formed. 'An examination was held yearly and the girl with the top marks became the Carnival Queen and was crowned at Langley Park [Huddersfield]. I got as far as a tie one year. Tuesday evenings I spent at the Co-op dancing class. I attended drama class on Thursdays . . . My grandmother and one or two relatives worked in the Co-op laundry.' The Co-op was indeed a way of life.

Gradually, with the emergence of small supermarkets and 'one-stop' shopping, the Co-op became dated. The dividend payment was replaced by stamps to be stuck in a book, which when full could be redeemed for cash or put towards the cost of further goods. A Bury man observed to me: 'The funny thing is that in 1990 most of our corner shops live on, in a fashion, mostly run by members of the Asian community.' But the supermarkets have triumphed.

10 A Mill Town Christmas

It's th'only time I sup spirits is Christmas an' new Year, exceptin' Saints Days an' when somebody offers me one. Otherwise, Ah'm abstemious.

Owd Thatcher, in a tale by T. Thompson

I was born in a very poor family. If we had a rabbit to eat, it was a luxury. We've had rabbit at Christmas.

An East Lancashireman

Ally, ally, aster –
Snow, snow faster!

A child with a sledge

He turned up at Woolworths, clad in red with cotton wool trimmings, and bearing scores of gifts, not one of which cost more than sixpence. The Father Christmas who mattered – the one who delivered the goods at home on Christmas Eve – was neither seen nor heard, though how he managed to negotiate our chimney without getting covered with soot, I could not fathom. An older lad said: 'It's your dad. I copped [caught] mine last Christmas. He knocked 'is toe on t'bed.' That lad was mistaken, of course. As was the Morley boy who yelled up the chimney: 'Fadder Kersmas! Fadder Kersmas! I want a train set!'

His mother said: 'Father Christmas isn't deaf.' The lad replied: 'I knaws that – but Grandfadder is!'

In due course, I realised that this was the greatest hoax in Christendom – that there were many Father Christmases, some with braces, some with holes in their socks, some – may heaven forgive them – with the stale tang of beer on their breath: and all spitting cotton wool from ill-fitting beards.

For me, and a million other housebound children, Christmas Eve was a time for deep sighing and for constant checks on the clock, which appeared to have stopped, or at least decided to go slow. Now and again there would be a woodpeckerish rap on the door, and children would be heard trying to persuade a householder that they had been singing carols.

Getting to sleep was difficult when a small boy's heart was pounding with excitement. A hush fell on the mill towns. If there was snow, the sounds of foot and wheel on the stone setts were muffled. But nothing could silence the voices of church and chapel folk, returning from special services, or of those other early celebrators (in the temporal sense). I heard the slurred voices of topers, whose unsteady progress would be recorded with terrifying clarity as marks on the snow. I tossed and turned in a hot bed, trying to adjust my heartbeat to the ticking of the bedside clock. I fell asleep through sheer exhaustion.

Came the frosty dawn of Christmas Day. It took a moment for the significance of the day to register. The bedroom was quiet and very cold. I shook a bed weakened by years of use as a trampoline. A responsive clumping sound from the bottom of the bed was reassuring. The pillow-case that last night hung flat and prim, having been freshly ironed, was now full of – who knows what? We didn't have our spoken wishes immediately granted, as they are today.

I slid out of bed, wincing as my feet encountered ice-cold linoleum, using light from a friendly neighbourhood street lamp to identify what Father Christmas had left . . . But I am 'getting ahead of myself', as an old friend says. In such circumstances, he adds: 'Unravel, lad, unravel.'

The run-down to Christmas began as early as October, when some of the wives had a special baking day. The house was flavoured by aromatic fruit loaves – the famous spicecakes – which were put away to ripen for the festive season. As already mentioned, the baking took place in ovens that were an integral part of the living room fireplace, and the fire was made to cook 'right slow'. A Brighouse octogenarian says:

> I always made two loaves; they were of the old-fashioned type with a lot of eggs, fruit and also lard, so they shone when they had been baked. They had to have time to 'come to'. If you cut them straight away, after baking, they would be hard. Keep them for a month or two and they 'soddened' themselves . . . I stored mine in a special way, putting greaseproof paper underneath and then wrapping them in a tea towel. I put the loaves in a large tin and stored it in the cellar. We had a right good, dry cellar. It was just the thing.

The Christmas puddings she made were not as fruity as the loaves. 'I made mine a week before I needed them, and I put sixpences and little fancy things, like bells and horseshoes, in each pudding. When they were "enough" I wrapped them in some fresh paper. On Christmas Day, a pudding was boiled till it was warmed through. We always had custard, not rum sauce, on our pudding.'

Between the world wars, on the hills around many of the mill towns stood farms on which turkeys and geese were reared for Christmas sale to those who could afford them. (The community also had its pig-keepers.) With the coming of December, the birds were given extra supplies of grain. There was nowt as tasteless as a green goose (one which had spent the whole of its brief life eating grass). Plucking geese was a tedious occupation. If it snowed, children chanted:

> They're plucking geese i' Scotland
> And sending t'feathers here . . .

The pigs died with a fearful squealing sound. They had at least enjoyed their last days, when they were 'crambed' with oatmeal balls and other foods to maximise the weight. All but the pig's squeal was saved; every scrap of flesh might be transformed by good cooking into a variety of interesting dishes.

Christmas at school brought some softening in the attitude of teachers, who normally penalised children for a sloppy posture, for cheek or for pranks – such as using a ruler, one end of which had been slipped in a crack of the desk, to propel ink-soaked blotting paper towards other scholars. The headmaster at my first school made sixpence available to each child. This sum must be spent at Woolworths, a type of store that had only just appeared. To a child who pondered hard and long about spending a penny, the notion of having a credit balance of SIXPENCE was breath-taking.

An essential prelude to Christmas at the chapel was a rendering of t'*Messiah*. In the heady days of great chapel choirs, the best-known oratorios were rendered according to season – Haydn's *Creation* in the New Year, Stainer's *Crucifixion* or *Olivet to Calvary* at Easter, and *Elijah* when 'th'Spirit took 'em'. Mill-owners liked their *Messiah* just before Christmas, cheerfully ignoring the fact that it had first been performed in Dublin at Easter.

Somewhere I have a quotation from Daniel Defoe about one of the old woollen towns of the West Riding. Defoe was such a good journalist, he was quite capable of writing about a place convincingly without having been there.

He did know the Halifax area well and referred to the local passion for the *Messiah*. Men going to and from the Cloth Hall, with rolls of cloth on their shoulders, would sing pieces from Handel's oratorio, and even the children lisped 'For unto us a Child is Born'. In East Lancashire, 'we had some of the best singers in the country as principals, you know. They got as good as they could get. Aye – and they'd talk for ages about how the different solos had been sung.' For some, it was effortless. Another would 'rive [tear] hissen to bits'. The *Messiah* season had to be well organised. 'They'd space 'em out so that they didn't land on th'same day.'

A traditional poem, 'At t'*Messiah*', divulges something of the 'plot':

They sang o' some sheep that hed getten astray
An' bi what I understood, they'd all gone a different way.
I don't know how many or how mich they cost
But that don't matter, t'main thing is – they were lost.

Then a young chap got up and sang bi hissen,
Whether they were his sheep that were lost I'm sure I can't tell.
But he said ivvery mountain an' hill wad be laid low.
Ah thowt they're bahn to find them sheep, choose what they do.

Then a young lass got up an' in a reight clear voice,
Shoo tell'd 'em they'd no need to sorrow but greatly rejoice.
It were a stiff piece, I'm sure it were hard work,
But shoo sang it as easy as if shoo were a lark . . .

And so on.

The organ at my Skipton chapel had been built with t'*Messiah* in mind. It rose to the height of a two-storey house in all the magnificence of tastefully decorated organ pipes and well polished woodwork. I earned my first shilling for 'playing' the organ, in the following way. A few weeks before *Messiah* was rendered – it was never actually sung, always 'rendered' – the organ-tuner arrived from Bannister's, the organ-makers with premises just a few miles down the valley. (Bannister's were famous organ people. I was once shown a grave in Kildwick churchyard where the headstone was in the form of one of their celebrated models.) I sat at the organist's stool. He placed one of my fingers on a key, and then vanished 'into the works', from which his resonant voice could be heard at irregular intervals shouting 'Next!', whereupon I shifted the finger to the next key . . .

Messiah day saw the Chapel packed. The first congregational hymn, 'Oh Come all ye Faithful', filled the air with wondrous sound. Every textile town in Yorkshire and Lancashire had one or more *Messiahs* 'with augmented choir'. The performances ranged from that in Huddersfield Town Hall, where there were massed ranks of choristers and orchestral back-up, to Mr and Mrs Churcher's annual presentation in t'tin tabernacle (it was made of corrugated iron) down Broughton Road at Skipton. Here, somehow, they managed to accommodate a choir, a few instrumentalists and a congregation. If it was raining, then the buckets which were strategically placed to collect drips from the rusting roof of the church had cloths placed in them to deaden the sound.

One year I chatted with an elderly chorister who had sung in chapel performances of Handel's oratorio for some forty years. She once performed in three different places in a single day. Her feat was excelled by a man living at T'Brigg (Hebden Bridge), where – so it was said – he was 'that struck' by Handel's work that he managed to hear parts of it four times in a single day. He rose early, and played part of the work on gramophone records; he heard a wireless version, and then attended a performance at a local chapel. In the evening, though it was snowing, he and two or three friends crossed the hills to hear a performance at Oxenhope!

It is related that a trumpeter in one mill town – a man weighing an impressive seventeen stone – would slip out of the chapel between his solos and imbibe at the nearest public house. And there was another who would tease the congregation, going through an elaborate cleaning routine with his trumpet as the minutes ticked by and the time for him to accompany 'The trumpet shall sound . . . ' drew nigh. A second or two – or so it seemed – before he was needed, he would pocket his handkerchief, and stand up and play the resounding first notes of the accompaniment.

From a seat at the back of the gallery at Skipton's Gargrave Road Chapel – a seat not recommended to sufferers from vertigo – I could see a mass of people. The choir's main strength lay in the soprano and bass sections. One or two rows of contraltos could be mustered, but few tenors turned up. There might only be a dozen, screeching their heads off to maintain some sort of musical balance. Two of us – young lads with gleaming faces and earnest expressions – were once permitted to sing among the sopranos. It was not a crime to be lost in the Amen Chorus; the crime was to be seen to be lost. The solemnity of the closing moments of *Messiah* was somewhat marred by the sight of two perplexed lads, feverishly trying to find their places in the book during a cascade of amens. I think we managed to remain silent for that earth-shattering pause just before the final notes. But the invitation was not repeated.

More often, there had been harmonious performances. At Bacup, in th'owd days: 'They could sing. You'd get hundreds of people, all singing in harmony. It meant something. If you were passing a chapel on *Messiah* Sunday, you stopped to listen.' I was always impressed by the number of choristers who had the scores with them and turned over pages with great regularity, but hardly ever looked at the notes. 'There wasn't a chapel round here [Bacup] where they could not have sung through t'oratorio without music. They were singing from memory.'

The Sunday School party, another pre-Christmas treat, was more like a glorified tea, but wearing good clothes and with knees shining bright I would join in the merriment in the warm schoolroom.

On Christmas Eve, traditionally, the Christmas singers were out and about. As a *Dalesman* reader once put it:

> An' we mun try oor best an' all,
> For t'bods [birds] deeant sing,
> There's nobbut us, on t'Birthday
> Morn, to greet
> The Heavenly King.

In more recent times, the church and chapel choirs would be doing their rounds. At Colne, 'there'd be half a dozen choirs. They sang in t'streets. You get none of it now.' Brighouse was toured by the choristers of Bridge End Chapel and those from Ebenezer Chapel at Bailiffe Bridge. 'If you woke up, you could listen to them; but nobody ever woke you up specially. Our parents liked you to sleep soundly on Christmas Eve.' At Saddleworth, on Christmas Eve, the Dobcross band toured the area in the middle of the night. 'They would come up the long drive to our big house and play on the terrace. I would wake up after midnight and hear the band playing "Hark the Herald Angels Sing". It was marvellous.'

Looking back, to boyhood, I sense that the run-up to Christmas was more enjoyable than the festival itself, when all we seemed to do was eat and burp. It could be very boring, visiting relatives or in turn receiving them. There was no television, of course, and no one would think of turning on the wireless when there was company.

Just before Christmas, my ambition switched from

being the owner of a sweet or toy shop to the occupation of grocer. Mincemeat, delivered to the corner shop in bulk, was dished out by a man wielding a knife. Looking back, as I left the shop, I would see him slowly, joyfully, removing the residue of mincemeat from the knife – with his tongue!

At Christmas-time, the menders at one West Riding mill took some sherry, mince pies and cake to work with them. They had a break for about an hour during the afternoon. This was not possible for the weavers, for the machines did not stop at their command. 'As you can imagine, they weren't reight suited when they saw what t'menders were doing.'

A rapping sound from t'attic in one Brighouse home was said to be made by Father, as he soled the children's shoes with 'little bits he'd cut off mill belting when he was repairing it'. In fact, he was also making toys – Christmas gifts for his own family and toys to sell to others to raise a little extra cash for the family's festivities.

In the mills, bunting draped the looms, the overlookers and tacklers risked lacerating their face muscles by smiling, and there was the odd sprig of mistletoe to bring a touch of romance into an unromantic setting. The Co-op had a Christmas tree. We had a Christmas tree, with baubles of time-honoured significance, though one or two of the delicate pieces were broken each year.

And now it was Christmas morning. The contents of the pillow-case were revealed – a few toys, a book, some fruit, some nuts and shining new pennies. Father Christmas must have been 'feeling the pinch'.

He was certainly not often seen in the mill towns late last century; conditions did improve, but workers had periodic onsets of austerity, when they were on short time or unemployed. One of those attending a soup kitchen, a common sight in 1926 in Lancashire towns, remarked: 'It's nobbut t'poor as helps t'poor.' Kindly folk made broth and soup, filling the basins of those in need; they cared especially for the children. Meat came from a friendly butcher who got cheap offal. Philanthropists – latter-day Father Christmases – distributed cast-off clothes, also clogs.

When people were really hard up, and it was a choice of food or fire, the fire was kept going to the extent of breaking up furniture as fuel. The proverb was: 'Last penny goes on th'fire.' In the meanest of homes, meals were always 'scratch' and the table never seemed to be cleared. 'They couldn't afford cow's milk as a rule. Nestlé's milk was the commonest kind.' Bread and jam were the staples. In the most poverty-stricken homes, it was mainly bread. For the very poor, therefore, Christmas could be a mockery. One mother pawned an old-fashioned sealskin coat to buy a few currants, a small wedge of cheese and oddments of other food, which she baked into small loaves. But they were not for the family. 'These is for them 'at comes in – understand?' she told her offspring. 'Don't dare ask for a bit or I'll skin yer! I'm not havin' you cryin' poverty!'

In the West Riding, pre-1914, Christmas feasting was not taken for granted. 'Mother might buy a box of dates and odd luxuries of that sort,' says a Brighouse man. One family who bought a hare at Christmas hanged it in the cellar until the New Year, by which time it was rather 'high'. Then they jugged it. A bottle or two of Guinness went into the brew.

A West Riding woman who specialised in minced meat at Christmas would buy a beast's heart, cook it, and cut it into small pieces, which she then placed in a wooden bowl. Her grandson recalls: 'We had a chopping knife which exactly fitted the curvature of this bowl. I had to chop, chop, chop away at the meat until my grandmother was satisfied, which she rarely was. She'd finish the job herself.'

Christmas, festival of light and laughter in the midst of

a murky winter, was a time when normal regulations about temperance were set aside; when, indeed, even a chapel-goer – if he could afford it – might have a wee drop o' something fiery, like sherry. Some people, let it be whispered, sipped something even stronger. A woman remarked to her neighbour: 'I saw your Bert t'other day. He wor suppin' whisky!' 'Nay,' said the embarrassed relative, 'wor it neat?' The first woman retorted: 'It wor broad dayleet!'

I cannot remember, in our Methodist household, anything stronger than the 'drop of something' poured into the Christmas pudding, just before the sixpences in their paper wrappings were put in, though grown-ups were expected to 'taste the cake', and some cheese, of course – plus a glass of sherry. Christmas was just about the only time of the year we opened a bottle.

During my years on the magazine *The Dalesman* I had two Christmases – one in August and a second at the usual time in December. August was the time when the Christmas issue was devised; when – in a heat wave, with ice cream from a cone dropping on to the copy– my mind would be ringing with 'Jingle Bells'. Long years ago, our Christmas issue was enlivened by an 'Under the Barber's Pole' tale from the Lancashire dialect writer, T. Thompson. He presented thoughts about the festival as spoken by the barber, his wife Sally, one Jim Gregson, 'Owd Thatcher' and 'Young Winterburn' – as follows.

When he was a lad, says the barber, his Christmas stocking contained an orange, an apple, 'a sugar pig wi' a red worsted tail, an' a tuppeny box o' chocolate creams'. He adds with grim irony: 'Banked up wi' cinders'. Then, when Sally mentions she has made a mince pie for each of them, Jim Gregson heartily approves. 'Kesmas,' he says, 'is the time for a bit o' gutsin'.' Owd Thatcher adds: ' . . . and suppin'.' Young Winterburn says, disapprovingly, 'It's nobbut an excuse for gormandisin'. Some on yo' fair makes a god o' yo're ballies [bellies].' Thatcher urges Young Winterburn to 'let thisel' goo a bit', adding: 'Get summat down thi chimbley [throat] while it's free.' But young Winterburn thinks that Christmas has become a pagan festival. 'Yo' should be down on yo'r knees instead o' sittin' up to th'table all th'time.' 'I hope to finish on me back,' retorts Owd Thatcher.

Better-off families tucked in to goose or turkey, with mince pie, followed at teatime by a gargantuan spread featuring brawn and meat pies. J.B. Priestley evoked Old Bradford in great style, harking back to the time when there was 'far less of this standardised *Merrie Yuletide* salesmanship, but a great deal more hearty and widespread enjoyment of the season itself.'

In 1987, I wrote to Priestley's widow and was given permission to prepare an anthology of his Yorkshire works. I set about my task with joy, first ransacking *Bright Day*, for his description of a Bruddersford Christmas, before the 1914–18 war shattered not only our social fabric but our peace of mind. Priestley had warm memories of his boyhood in the home of his schoolmaster father. Christmas was about people, not things. He wrote of bands and choirs, of the incessant round of relatives' and friends' houses, of the consumption of 'acres of rich pound cake and mince-pies' washed down 'by cataracts of old beer and port, whisky and rum; the air was fragrant and rich with cigar smoke, as if the very mill chimneys had taken to puffing them.'

One Christmas, a West Riding lass borrowed her father's stocking to attach to the bottom of her bed. 'His stockings were big ones!' The mill town children of half a century and more ago expected little, and so were not disappointed when the stocking at the bottom of the bed contained only an orange, a rosy apple, a new penny, some nuts and a toy of some sort. 'If I didn't get a toy, it would be a book.'

Christmas dinner in a typical terraced house was not turkey (which no average family could afford) nor goose (unless someone had been able to barter successfully at the market late on Christmas Eve, when bargains abounded). The meat was often 'a bit o' this' or 'a bit o' that'. At one house, where mother, father and seven children sat down to pork, there was no starter 'except some pop', and the main course was followed by Christmas pudding and custard. Tea would include Christmas cake with cheese, mince pie 'and a sandwich of some sort'. Tinned salmon, as mentioned earlier, was a special treat. 'We broke the salmon up, took the bones out and the skin off, and got a slice of bread and rubbed it, dropping the crumbs on to the salmon. We then put in an egg we had whisked and we added salt and pepper and vinegar. The salmon was put in sandwiches.'

On Boxing Day the children played, and on the following day the brief Christmas holiday was over for the workers. The buzzers sounded and looms began to clatter again.

The next spell of excitement came with New Year's Day, when the youth of Skipton – hundreds of lads and some lassies – went 'scrambling'. For a few hours, the town's traffic was disrupted by what today would be called a rampaging mob. No damage was caused, and most shopkeepers who looked out at the sea of expectant faces and heard the roar of anticipation, could but hurl out cash or kind. A new year opened for some with bruised fingers, gashed legs and ripped clothes.

11   Not at Work

Religious folk didn't even 'garden' on a Sunday. Irreligious folk dug in their allotments.

A chapel-goer at Burnley

We had one trade union member — and a more disinterested unionist it would be hard to find.

A mill-owner at Morton, near Keighley

We were a 'chapil' family. Chapel folk had a simple, homely religion. They didn't have a great deal of time for 'middle men'. Each person felt he had a direct line to the Almighty.

Grannie was Church of England – though she didn't often go to church. Auntie Annie, who did, set a great deal of store by respectability and didn't like the way the Nonconformists showed their feelings, though the days were long past when a sinner was dangled over Hell's fires or an over-stimulated worshipper might kick out the back of the pew in front of him.

Church and Chapel did offer a variation on the mill town theme of 'bed and work'. The stones of which they were fashioned had been hewn from the same quarries as those which built the mills. The Protestant ethic, solid as a rock – that the way to heaven lay through unrelenting work – was evident in both, though perhaps more so in the Chapel, where many of the mill-owners played a prominent part, some to the extent of actually building places of worship, as I mentioned in chapter 5. Perhaps some of them saw it as an insurance policy for the Hereafter.

Nonconformity turned out 'characters' by the hundred. These were people of original thought and behaviour, the possessors of a simple but strong faith. It was said of one convert, that during a class meeting he confided in the leader that 'people think I'm cracked'. The leader promptly prayed: 'Crack a few more, Lord, there's plenty o' work for 'em down here!'

A chapel-goer was noted for his/her sobriety. No one drank, gambled or swore. 'Father was a good-living chap; we were not even allowed to have a pack of cards.' In the mill towns and villages, before the 1914–18 war, only transport workers, postmen and milkmen worked on the first day of the week. 'Sundays were for "best suits", for chapel, church, Sunday School and – if you didn't support any of these – for pubs.' Respectable folk did not even read Sunday newspapers. A West Riding octogenarian recalls:

We were never allowed to do anything on a Sunday, only read. We were not even allowed to knit. My sister never went to church; one Sunday she went off to her boy friend's house. I was five years younger than she was. I was on Bradford Road, chatting to the boy I eventually married, and she came up and saw me. She fetched me such a side-winder [blow] because I hadn't been to church. I was eighteen at the time, but I didn't say anything about it when I got home.

On Sunday, long years ago, men exchanged clogs for boots and cloth caps for bowler hats. Those women who habitually wore clogs and shawls on their working days would not dream of donning them on Sunday. At Whitsuntide, the time for new clothes, families came forth from their homes with all the glamour of emergent butterflies.

I used to have a straw bonnet, decorated with rosebuds or violets. I had new underclothes, new dress, new shoes. It was called 'Sunday best'. At Whitsuntide what you had been wearing became 'best wear' for Saturday. And so on . . . I remember going to Sunday School in my new clothes. The minute I got home, I had to take them off and put on something older. After dinner, I'd put on the Sunday clothes again and be in Sunday School by two o'clock. When I got home at three o'clock, I had to change once again, unless we went for a walk.

Many tales were told of chapel folk. When a Methodist became ill, the doctor provided him with medicine. On his next visit, the doctor asked the wife: 'Does your husband take his medicine religiously?' She replied: 'Nay, doctor – he cusses every time I give 'im some.'

At chapel, the big pulpit, in its central position, emphasised the importance of extempore preaching. Chapel folk accepted the Bible without qualification. A man at the industrialised village of Carleton, near Skipton, disliked arguments about religion. When such an argument broke out, he would say: 'If t'Good Book's reight, it's reight; if not, clap [throw] it at t'back o' t'fire!' And the story is told of two Bradford scrap merchants who built up a lucrative business. One man was 'converted'. His brother said: 'It's made a world of difference to him; he's always happy and he loves doing things for other people . . . I've thowt many a time I'd like to get missen "converted". Then I've thought to missen – if that 'appens, there's nobody left to weigh t'scrap.'

Everyone respected the Salvation Army because they didn't hesitate to mix religion with daily life. We knew a songster leader – a nice little chap who worked at one of the mills. A Yeadon woman who had been 'saved' by the

Army set about knitting 'religious' dresses and pullovers in Fair Isle. Emblazoned across them in purple or red were the words, 'God is Love'. As a small boy, I went to magic lantern shows at the Citadel, and would stare at a large wooden bench (centre, front) because on it was written 'Mercy Seat'. It was where the penitents knelt. We went to see the cavortings of a fictitious bear called Rupert, to hear a short talk – and then, excitedly, to queue up for bags of sweets before we left for home.

In the mill towns, many a parish church had a steeple, as though to compete with the high chimneys of the mills. Chapels came in all shapes and sizes, from the little missions to those where t'bosses went – big, ornate buildings, with adjacent school premises that were almost as large. The smaller chapels bore such names as Hebron, Salem, Bethesda, Ebenezer, Providence, Paradise and Zion. Of the larger premises, which were not unlike Anglican churches, was St John's Methodist Church in Bradford. It was opened in 1879 and replaced a wooden school building. St John's had seating for a thousand people.

It was a matter of pride, when a new chapel was opened, that it should be 'free of debt'. The mill-owner who was one of the 'pillars' of the chapel paid his workers miserably but managed to find quite large sums to keep the chapel solvent. The kitty was augmented annually by the proceeds of a bazaar. Collections made at special services helped to defray expenses.

Chapels vied with each other as to the size of the collections on such as *Messiah* Sunday. Chapels of various denominations had their versions of Handel's great work. At one chapel, as the echoes faded on the last triumphal A–m–e–n, and before the minister pronounced the benediction, the door of the vestry opened and a steward appeared with a slip of paper in his hand. With great dignity, he mounted the steps into the pulpit and beheld the capacity crowd. 'Friends,' he announced with another glance at the paper. 'The grand total of the collections today is [a pause for absolute quietness] £120.' No one applauded, of course, because this was a chapel. The steward added: 'And that's £10 more than Ebenezer, £20 more than t'Baptists and £22 more than t'Congregationalists.'

It had been a thoroughly good 'do'.

I knew a mill-owner who managed to serve God and Mammon simultaneously. He had a busy mind and, wherever he happened to be, was forever remembering business matters. He was in chapel for each service. So was the young lady who was his secretary at the mill. If he 'bethought hissen' during the service, he might signal to the young lady, who would promptly leave the choir pew and join him in the schoolroom, where he would dictate a letter. No one complained, of course. Mill brass kept this chapel going! Some chapels were known locally, if not officially, after their donors or principal supporters. At the industrialised village of Cononley in the Aire Valley I have taken services at what was known locally as Green's Chapel (Methodist) and, on another day, at Reddihough's Chapel (Baptist).

After the service, Mr Reddihough was pointed out as my host for tea. I beheld a small, pleasant man and pictured being led to a cottage with a garden gate adorned by a honeysuckle arch. Instead, he led me to the front of the chapel, where stood a chauffeur-driven Rolls-Royce. Mr Reddihough, a wealthy man, was well known in West Riding textile circles. We were driven across the valley to an ancient hall. I remember sitting alone in a large panelled room, where a diversion was provided by a count of the wooden mice – indicating that the woodwork had been carved at Kilburn, in the shadow of the Hambleton Hills, by the celebrated Robert Thompson, who used a mouse as his trademark.

Our chapel, at Skipton, was under the patronage of a burly mill-owner who, at the start of a sermon, distributed sweets wrapped in crinkly paper to all and sundry. He developed a loud, dry cough if the service took more than an hour. This was the celebrated Tom Lumb, a man whose gruff manner belied a generous nature.

When, as a preacher, I began to take services in mill town chapels, I could be overawed by their size and importance in local life. At the small industrialised village of Kelbrook, twixt Skipton and Colne, was a grandiose chapel indeed. Here I was led from the vestry, through echoing schoolrooms, to the door leading into the chapel. I expected to see about twenty people, but the place was full, for it was an anniversary occasion, and behind me were row after row of the Colne Orpheus Choir.

On Sunday, a great hush descended on the mill towns. Machinery was inactive. Mill fires dozed. Few children went out to play. If you washed and hung out clothes on the Sabbath, you were surely courting disaster and would be struck by the next available thunderbolt. One lady chapel-goer, recalling a time when illness in the family decreed that washing should be done on Sunday, said: 'I half expected, as I hung out clothes, to hear a voice from above the clouds telling me not to do it.'

Families – decked in their best clothes – made for the innumerable places of worship. New clothes, the hallmark of respectability, were usually purchased in the spring of the year because it was then that the Co-op paid out the divi.

Early this century, no less than a third of the urban population had some association with the Christian religion. There was considerable rivalry between chapels, even between Methodist chapels, and in the old days a mill-owner who did not get his own way at one would set up another. It is related that two stewards who were on duty in the porch of a chapel where an organ had just been installed, replacing a harmonium, informed two members of another chapel who were passing: 'We've getten an organ.' The rejoinder was: 'All tha wants now is a monkey.' As quick as lightning came the reply: 'Aye, an' all thou wants is an organ.'

One of my favourite Congregationalists told of a zealous young lay preacher who, arriving at the chapel where he was to take the service, saw people milling about on the pavement outside. Thinking that he could save time by shaking them by the hand before the service, he did so – only to realise that he had just made a fuss of a bus queue!

Among the 'Sweet Singers of Zion', as someone referred collectively to old-time preachers, were Congregationalists, Baptists, Unitarians and Methodists. Someone wrote of the most evangelistic of them: 'They stoked up your fears, they embellished your hopes, they had a sort of "no holds barred" attitude towards religion.' Methodism, which was numerically superior, had its own Three R's – Ruin, Redemption, Regeneration.

The Nonconformists could certainly sing. Among the best-known and loved tunes were 'Rimington' and 'Deep Harmony'. The name of the first is that of a village within easy viewing range of Pendle Hill. The tune was composed by Francis Duckworth, whose family had moved to Colne, where he became a successful grocer and also organist at the Albert Road Chapel.

'Rimington', published in 1904 in the heyday of religious gatherings, was sung for the first time at the Colne Whitsuntide processions, to the hymn with which it has been most strongly associated: 'Jesus shall reign where'er the sun'. Some twenty thousand people sang it on one occasion in Nelson. It became a special favourite with bandsmen, and featured in some early broadcasts. Its appeal to missionary organisations ensured its worldwide popularity.

To several generations of West Riding folk, 'Deep Harmony' was a very special hymn tune, used widely by choirs and brass bands. The famous Black Dyke Mills Band popularised it by playing the tune after every concert. At its most celebrated period, 'Deep Harmony' was recorded on gramophone records and played fairly often, by special request, on 't'wireless'. For me, it evokes images of the old West Riding, with its mills, chapels and countless amateur music-makers.

Handel Parker, its composer, was born at Oxenhope, in a family with strong Haworth connections. Nearly all the Parkers were musical. Handel's father, Abraham, was an exponent of the clarinet and the violin; he sang tenor. His daily work was that of coachman to the mill-owner William Greenwood. Handel's mother, Martha, had been christened at Haworth in 1825 by the Rev. Patrick Brontë. Her fine voice did not desert her until her dying day, at the age of 85. She sang for the doctor attending her in her last illness and is reported to have 'hit the top notes'.

Abraham and Martha named their children after individuals who had become famous in the musical world – Handel (the first-born), Miriam, Jubal, Haydn, Frederick and Sarah. (Frederick was to have been christened Mozart, but according to Lavinia, Handel's daughter, his mother changed the name when a neighbour said it sounded like 'Noah's Ark'!)

As a small boy Handel practised on the harmonium by candlelight long after his parents had gone to bed. At the age of seven, he was playing the flute in the Oxenhope Drum and Fife Band. In the following year he was at the harmonium in the Haworth Baptist Sunday School. Two years later he obtained his first appointment as an organist.

Handel Parker started work in t'mill, being taught wool-sorting at the firm of William Greenwood, Oxenhope. Lavinia related of her father that 'he sorted the first bale of mohair that came to England'.

He was aged 20 when he left the mill for a full-time musical career, which was to span more than 60 years. In the joint role of organist and choirmaster, he served Methodist and Congregationalist chapels over a wide area.

'Deep Harmony' was composed in 1867, nearly 40 years before it was first published. When it was recorded as a gramophone record by Besses o' th'Barn Band, the conductor, Alec Owen, referred to the tune's 'stately sonorousness in majesty and symmetry.' In 1932 alone it was included in at least 500 brass band programmes, and was also selected for massed band concerts at the leading festivals, such as Crystal Palace, Leicester and Edinburgh.

When I began looking for information about Handel Parker and his great hymn, I found to my astonishment that, although he died as long ago as 1928, on his 74th birthday, some close relatives are still alive. The oldest of them, Nellie Hardaker, of Thornton, a niece of the composer, has celebrated her 90th birthday. She remembers him as tall and thin, with a natty moustache. 'You couldn't call him good-looking, but he had a kind face.' He also had what a picture cannot reveal, a kind disposition, especially towards the large family of his brother Frederick, who attained the responsible job of manager at the stone quarries at Cullingworth but died at the early age of 48. Frederick's widow was left with 13 children and yet, like her contemporaries, was too proud to accept 'charity'. Handel Parker was able to find excuses to give money – even a half sovereign on one occasion – to the children, knowing they would promptly hand it over to their mother.

Handel himself made scarcely anything out of his hymn-writing, and he died a relatively poor man. The funeral service was in Shipley Parish Church where, in accordance with Handel Parker's wish, a combined choir sang two hymns to music he had composed. One was a setting of 'Abide with Me'; the other was, of course, Isaac Watts's great hymn 'Sweet is the Work' to the tune – 'Deep Harmony'.

The chapel choirs were often fortunate to be led by men of humour as well as character. One Yorkshire choirmaster, speaking during a rehearsal for Stainer's *Crucifixion*, said: 'Nah then, lads – let's have "Fling wide the Gates" just once more. An' think on – doan't hod 'em oppen sa long this time.' Another choirmaster, during a rehearsal of the finer points of Handel's *Judas Maccabaeus*, said irritably: 'You mak me want ter say stuff as I shouldn't say in t'chapel. You stand theer like a lot o' gaslamps wi' t'leets out.'

Walter Bennett recorded that at Nelson, one of the smaller towns, in 1901 nine Sunday Schools produced 4,500 scholars; in 1923, the figures were 21 and 6,000; in 1931, a total of 21 schools yielded 3,400 scholars.

All the same, the chapels could still impress their locality at Whitsuntide, when it was the habit to go the rounds of the relatives, each of whom was expected to admire the customary new clothes and slip a copper (usually a penny) into a child's pocket. 'Let's see if I've something, love,' said an auntie. And I couldn't get out of the house quick enough to remove that 'something' from my pocket. Wearing a new suit was a frustrating business, anyway. Every move was scrutinised by Ma. She did not want to see it misused for an instant.

Whitsuntide was the occasion of an annual stocktaking, in the form of the Whitsuntide Walk, mentioned earlier, when banners fluttered, bands played and half a town's population was on parade while the other half looked on. At Nelson, 'the processions set off from the different churches, each party having its large banners, and then you'd get this sudden, dramatic convergence on the centre of town'. At the end of the day, each child received a bag of sweets and a new rubber ball, also vast quantities of currant buns and coffee, served at long trestle tables set out in a handy field.

The Catholics walked in the morning. The 'rest' perambulated during the afternoon. The Nonconformists of Skipton ended their procession outside the Town Hall, where hymns were sung. The Anglicans continued into church. One year, as the two groups separated, we were singing:

> We are not divided –
> All one body, we . . .

But the chapels, by and large, were becoming introverted, and chapel life began to wither. Two world wars broke the succession, and greater affluence and mobility provided alternative attractions.

The Church of England never seemed to have its numerical and spiritual ups and downs; it plodded on, sure of its authentic foundation and sure, too, of its destiny. At St John's, Horbury, is a framed letter from the Rev. Sabine Baring-Gould, who was at one time curate-in-charge. The letter states that 'Onward, Christian Soldiers' was written here at Whitsuntide, 1865. Baring-Gould said it took him merely fifteen minutes to write the hymn, which is sung to a popular tune by Sir Arthur Sullivan.

For a time, there was little difference between religion and the new politics being proclaimed by religious-minded people. Grandfather, a pioneer Socialist, did not have a bomb-making factory in his cellar. He was a devoted Primitive Methodist, with a simple but unwavering faith. Socialism would attain its objectives when people realised how rotten was the old system; socialism would certainly not be brought in by force.

At nearby Keighley, during the heady 1890s when Socialists were bestirring themselves, Philip Snowden, the man who was to become Chancellor in Ramsay MacDonald's National Government of 1931, was making his reputation on political platforms. 'Our Philip', a native of Cowling and a passionate young radical, was associated with the Independent Labour Party, founded in Bradford in 1893. Someone once described ILP speeches as being 'a blend of religion and sentiment'. Snowden put up for Blackburn. A political commentator at Blackburn wrote:

> He brought to politics something of the emotional qual-
> ity of religion. The weavers of Blackburn crowded to
> his meetings, held by the spell of his oratory, and
> although he had no party organisation to help him, and
> no party funds, and was the representative of a party
> which seemed to consist of a few wild voices crying in
> the wilderness, he put up a fierce and memorable fight.

Philip was unpretentious. Addressing the Press Club in London in 1932, he reminded his hearers that he had often been criticised by the Press for his pronunciation of certain words. He told of the southern schoolmistress who took up a job in Yorkshire and immediately came up against the use of the vernacular in everyday conversation. The teacher declared: 'Tom has putten putten where he should have putten put.'

Nelson sent a strong delegation to a suffrage procession. Before they entrained, a photograph was taken at the railway station. The women had enhanced their femininity by wearing their smartest clothes and broadest hats. Selina Cooper (1864–1946) became known as the Nelson suffragette. She was a 'respectable rebel', and did not chain herself to railings.

Anyone who stepped into the political arena needed to be physically as well as mentally resilient. When Dan Irving, the first Burnley man to become a Socialist of significance, switched his allegiance from Labour to the Tories, it caused a local sensation. It happened at the second of two meetings attended by Lord Derby. An old Quaker friend recalls of that occasion: 'My dad was standing on a stool at the back of the Mechanics' Hall. He called out something, and he got thrown down the thirteen steps outside. He hit every one of those steps and lost his new hat. He'd paid 6s 9d for the hat that very morning.'

At the beginning of this century, Tories tended to be the superior industrialists and the leaders of local political life. But many of the mill towns were heavily committed to the Liberal cause, which derived support from mill-owners as well as working-class folk. One keen Liberal thought nothing of walking from Littletown to Cleckheaton to hear the declaration of a poll, however late the hour. And when Lloyd George visited Huddersfield, he spoke in a packed football ground.

In the past, textile workers seem to have been more Tory-minded than Labour-minded. A peculiar situation arose between union members in Blackburn, when some decided they did not want to give any money to the Labour Party. So they formed their own union, called the Protection Society – nicknamed the Tory Club. The Blackburn and district Weavers', Winders' and Warpers' Association became known as the Labour Club. Much later, they merged.

Grim struggles developed in the 1920s. When the General Strike was declared, the loyalty of many working folk to bosses who had been considerate towards them was evident, firstly in the small number of union members recruited, and secondly in the many places where full production was maintained.

In winter, nearly every active lad played football; and large crowds would hasten, in an orderly fashion, to the home games of the celebrated Rugby League teams. In fact, football was a mill town obsession. As a small boy, visiting relatives at Burnley, I recall winter afternoons at their home on Pike Hill when an enormous roar attended every goal scored by the home side. Another Saturday saw us watching Rugby League at Keighley. The variety of sporting events in the mill towns was impressive. In winter, there was also the sporting activity that circulated around the pubs and clubs, but this tended to be not much more exacting than dominoes and darts. 'We played billiards at the Church Institute – then you had to be content with a cup of tea.'

In summertime, many lads joined cricket teams. I remember, from my boyhood, watching cricket matches being held against a backdrop of mills. The sight of white flannels against black stone was to form an enduring mental picture. The Tanner family of Greenfield invited a Yorkshire team to visit the local ground at the end of the season, about September, 'in the days when a cricketer got about £10 a match.' To go to Saddleworth, to have a free meal and to socialise, then turn out against the village team, was considered to be great fun.'

Geoffrey Moorhouse has written about the 'competitive fire' of league cricket as played in the North. Of the Roses Matches, 'the greatest of all tussles between county rivals', Neville Cardus wrote that such cricketing events 'remain coloured by imagination in a frieze of memory set against a grim and humorous background of North of England life'. It was not so much humour, but wit. Cardus was at Old Trafford when Sutcliffe stonewalled for half an hour. The silence was finally broken by a voice: "Erbert, coom on; what dost tha think thou is, a –– war memorial?'

My great uncle, W.H. Cartman (1861–1935), rose to the dizzy cricketing heights of having a place in the Yorkshire side; he played four matches for Yorkshire in 1891 and then was dropped because, as I understand it, he aroused the displeasure of the captain, Lord Hawke, the quintessential Yorkshireman – who, let it be whispered, was born in Lincolnshire.

Yorkshire has had its many cricketing heroes, such as Percy Holmes and Herbert Sutcliffe, Len Hutton and Wilfred Rhodes, Tom Emmett and Maurice Leyland, Hedley Verity and Bill Bowes. And every West Riding schoolboy knows of Hutton's most magnificent achievement – 364 not out, a world record, achieved at the Oval while batting for 13 hours 20 minutes. The Yorkshire Club was formed in 1863 and its eventual home, Headingley, came on the market in 1888, when it was Lot 17a in the disposal of the Cardigan Fields estate. It was on this ground, in August 1977, that Geoff Boycott became the first player to complete a century of centuries in a Test Match.

Lancashire heroes included A.C. Maclaren, A.H. Hornby, J.T. Tyldesley, J.B. Statham and Cyril Washbrook. Statham, a native of Gorton, Manchester, played for Lancashire in 430 matches between 1950 and 1968, and in thirteen seasons he took 100 wickets. Washbrook, born in 1914, played five hundred matches for Lancashire between 1933 and 1959. With Len Hutton he formed England's opening pair in the Tests immediately after the war. On seventeen occasions in England, Washbrook hit 1000 runs in a season (twice, the number exceeded 2000). Stories about Yorkshire and Lancashire are legion. They include one about a Lancashire side that was playing against Cambridge University. The Lancashire bowler asked a player he knew to be the son of an official of the county club: 'What do you want, sir? A full toss? Or a long walk on the leg side?'

An elderly man, one of the wool salesmen visiting Saddleworth mills each Monday, was a great supporter of Yorkshire cricket. A retired mill director recalls: 'When I was a young man, in 1928, he took me to watch Yorkshire play against Lancashire at Old Trafford. We travelled by train to Manchester Exchange. Who should be in the same carriage but a man who was introduced to me as – Maurice Leyland! He had just been selected to go to Australia.'

Nonconformity had greatly improved the musical taste of the people. It is a matter of widespread pride that Delius was born in Bradford. As a boy, he rode a pony across the moors to Ilkley, yet he took the first opportunity to escape from milldom to the warm, sunlit landscape of France.

The mill-towners still enjoy 'a good brass band' – witness the packed audiences in town halls when some celebrated band arrives to provide an evening of lively music. The old brass bands had their band clubs which were also 'drinking dens'. Beer was a prime attraction. Phil Smith met a chap who told him:

> If a fellow disrupted a band through drinking, then no action was taken against him. His value was considered in relation to how much he spent over the bar . . . We went to London in 1924. On the Friday night, we had a bit of a rehearsal and then the lads spread out and went their own ways. Some of them went down Soho and had a night on the binge.
>
> There was one chap who had so much that by the time Saturday morning came, he couldn't play his part. And he had a leading part for about sixteen bars. It was terrible. There was another who, on his way back from Soho to his 'digs', stuffed bottles of beer into the case he used to carry his instrument. When he came to play it, Saturday morning, valves wouldn't work.

'Saddleworth Band contest at Whitsuntide was famous. It was Trinity, actually – we didn't bother about Whitsuntide at Saddleworth. I remember when Black Dyke, Faireys, the Co-op – thirty or forty bands, including the locals, played in various outdoor venues, before large crowds.' A pause for breath. Then: 'The beer drinking that went on was unbelievable.'

12   Seaside and the Dales

When you went out on t'prom at Blackpool, in Wakes Week, you might just as well have stopped at Colne. You knew everybody.
A mill worker's holiday recollection

It was good to see some ordinary mill girls who'd saved up, and were determined to enjoy themselves at Blackpool, hiring a horse cab to go to Yates's Wine Lodge for port and lemon.
A Burnley memory

At holiday time, Blackpool held the major appeal for Lancashire families. The resort had evolved to cater for the urban masses. Everybody who went on holiday from East Lancashire finished up at Blackpool, Morecambe or Southport, but mainly at Blackpool. 'You knew everybody on the train.'

Blackpool, which in 1789 was a modest sea-bathing resort, and sixty years later was so small as to be unremarkable, blossomed from the arrival of the railway. Its Victorian growth was astonishing. The Central and North Piers were built in the 1860s. A century later, the Winter Gardens were offering under-cover entertainment to cheat the northern weather. Blackpool Tower, opened in 1894, gave the place a Continental flavour, the idea being derived from the success of the Eiffel Tower. The iron tower, 518 feet high, could be seen from afar across the flat Fylde landscape. A holiday had truly begun when someone on the train saw its distinctive candlestick form and shouted: 'There's the Tower!' Its iron legs straddled an entertainment complex.

Blackpool was never too proud to pinch good ideas. The Tower Ballroom, built on lines similar to those of the Paris Opera House, was opened for business in 1899. Blackpool Illuminations, which were first seen in 1897 when five brightly lit tramcars ran up and down the front, were inspired by the celebrations held in Berlin for the Kaiser's birthday! Blackpool also knew how to 'pack 'em in'. And nobody objected to the crush. In 1919, some ten thousand people from Nelson alone stayed at Blackpool for at least four days. They strolled along the half-mile stretch of front known – with typical Blackpool cheek – as the Golden Mile; they bought paper caps on which was printed 'Kiss me Quick'; they danced to the strains of the organ in the fantastic Tower Ballroom, and they went to shows on the piers. There was novelty in being out on an iron limb, above the restless tide.

In St Anne's, an exclusive part of the Blackpool district, were to be found, as mentioned earlier, some of the fine detached houses of mill-owners, both active and retired. Southport's appeal was its splendid sands, stretching away to infinity. It was not every day that the tide managed to cross them. In 1919, about a thousand Nelson people – a tenth of the number that had opted for Blackpool – headed for Southport. Another holiday venue, which that year attracted five hundred people, was the Isle of Man, for which you sailed from Fleetwood.

One clogger and his wife, who lived near Rochdale and earned rather more than the average wage, impressed the neighbours by holidaymaking at Torquay, which brought the desired 'Ee! Nivver!' response from those living round about, to whom Torquay was 'somewhere down south'.

Bradford folk made a special fuss about Morecambe. So much West Riding 'brass' was used in its development,

and so popular did it become with the residents of Wooltopolis, that it became known as Bradford-by-the-Sea. A
woolman could, if he wished, live at Morecambe, catching
the resi (residential train) to and from Forster Square in
Bradford. We – the ordinary folk of Skipton – travelled by
ordinary train. Mill town holidays were staggered, but
congestion was unavoidable when a high proportion of
townsfolk moved, lemming-like, to the coast. They did so
at their own expense, for there were no holidays with pay
until the late 1930s.

Stations were dingy, smelling of fish and soot. As the
train approached, small children would be drawn well
back from the platform edge, 'or you'll get sucked into
the engine'. The holiday might be said to have begun
when the train for Morecambe drew out of the platform
and, gaining speed, produced that rhythmic clatter – *dé-
de-de, dum* – as it travelled between wondrously green
fields dotted with clean sheep. As a mill-towner of tender
years, I remember the ecstasy of leaving Morecambe
station for t'prom and a wide-angle view of the Bay. What
many people said was ozone – 'it's supposed to be good
for thee' – was rotting seaweed. The gulls uttered laughing cries as they circled; and they appeared to me to laugh
louder as they deposited some white stuff on the visitors,
who thereafter engaged in surreptitious dry-cleaning.

The seaside ritual was unchanging. A mill town family
went to long-remembered 'digs'. On the train journey,
there would be excited talk among friends about the various boarding houses, with their romantic names and 'sea
views' that did not exist. 'Yon crow, on th'chimla, is t'only
thing round here that's getten a sea view,' some wag
would declare.

The Wakes Week experience – this glorious release from
serfdom in the mills – included buying saucy postcards
and sandy sandwiches; making sand-castles adorned with
paper flags; and having donkey rides, attended by the
jangle of bells on the reins and a churned-up feeling in the

rider's stomach. Children watched Punch get his come-uppance, and Aunt Dora shrieked with enjoyment as she dipped her bare feet in the flow tide. The Morecambe tides were said to move in and out with the speed of a good horse. When the Bay was a damp desert, it teemed with people; then the flow tide overwhelmed the shallow Bay, performing pincer movements around the sand-banks, smacking its lips against the sea defences.

The walker on the 'prom' saw human life in its most varied forms – the middle-aged spinster, looking sad as she attended her elderly mother among a throng of bois-terous holidaymakers. Maiden aunts, who sat in wind-cheating shelters, moved their eyes as restlessly as spec-tators at Wimbledon, determined to 'miss nowt' and pre-tending to be shocked if they saw anything naughty.

The sounds of Holiday Morecambe included the *kleep*, *kleep* of those pied dandies, the oyster-catchers, and the cries of the big gulls: those incessant laughing cries. They appeared to be rejoicing at having plastered yet another luckless holidaymaker. A seaside holiday meant an abun-dance of sand in which to dig. At Morecambe, sand was mixed with a little estuarial mud, as I discovered when castle-building. One lass from a Lancashire town was frus-trated because her father – a pillar of the chapel – would not let her go on the beach on Sunday. It was not con-sidered seemly for a Christian to do that. 'Can I go if I make sand-chapels instead of sand-castles?' the girl asked in exasperation.

To me, Morecambe meant little boarding houses where each table had a cruet and where guests, assembling in the lounge just before the time for the evening meal, looked as restless as vultures waiting for their next gob-bets of food. It was just the same at Blackpool. Wilfred Pickles was fond of telling the story of the mill town lad whose speech was so loud and broad his mother felt embarrassed in the company of her new friends.

As the family sat around their table in the dining room,

awaiting a meal, the small boy opened his mouth, and mother sensed that he was about to ask to go to the toilet. She whispered: 'Go upstairs, love. You know where it is.' He went upstairs. The quiet, ultra-polite dining room talk was resumed, with everyone talking posh. Then the shrill voice of the boy was heard from upstairs. 'Mum!!!' She could not evade the need to reply. Going to the dining room door, she yelled: 'What, luv?' Silence for a few seconds. Then, from the small, private room upstairs came the cry: 'I can see t'Tower while I'm on t'closet!'

For some visitors, an illusion would be shattered as a small girl, wearing a pretty floral dress and with a neat, starched bow of matching fabric in her hair, looked from the lounge window and (with tormented vowels) commented on the weather: 'It's chucking it dahn!' And there was the Burnley woman with 'fancy ideas' who began her account of a holiday in Southport with the words, spoken in plum-in-the-mouth tones: 'We walked out of the station and looked around – and [the strain was telling] we was fair capped [amazed].'

A holiday in Blackpool represented a considerable financial outlay for those working at the mills. Albert Smith, a mill boss at Brighouse, briefly lectured anyone who took up an office job: 'Sethee, if tha behaves thisen; that is, if tha does what tha's telled wi'aht bein' to tell twice, I'll put thrippence a week in t'Holiday Club for thi – soas tha can hev a day trip to Blackpool.'

At Easter, the first holiday break of the year, the mills closed for a couple of days. In years long gone, when hardly anyone had a car, Easter saw a mass invasion of favourite picnic areas not far from town. The perceptive J.B. Priestley wrote: 'The moors, to the West Riding folk, are something more than a picnic place, a pretty bit of local countryside. They are the grand escape.'

One such place was Shipley Glen, with its rack railway and refreshment hut. The escape route for thousands was through Bingley and Eldwick to Dick Hudson's and the moorland trod leading to Ilkley. The thought of having a cool drink at that grey stone pub beside the moors – a pub more properly called The Fleece Inn, High Eldwick – was the motivation that many a mill worker would find adequate when contemplating the ascent of that long hill from Bingley. The celebrated Dick Hudson presided over the Fleece from 1850 until 1878. He succeeded his father, Thomas, who had become the tenant in 1809 and had also served as the constable at Bingley. Dick was in turn succeeded by his son, John, who maintained the family connection until his death in 1893.

This moor-edge pub still provides drinks and good food. A century ago, working-class families from the nearby textile towns would arrive in droves and dine on ham and eggs, which, over the Easter week-end, were being served from 6 a.m. until 11 p.m., using a famous eighteen-inch frying pan. The home-fed ham being fried was said to scent the air as far as Eldwick village, and caused wanderers over the moor to 'twitch their noses like camels coming to water and to lengthen their stride for the last quarter of a mile'. In Victorian days, a helping of roast beef and Yorkshire pudding cost a shilling a head. Or you might have a ploughman's lunch for tuppence!

Dick Hudson's, like many country inns at that time, incorporated a farm. 'Falling into bed at 2 a.m., the staff were up four hours later to serve the first customer and to feed the livestock.' The annual pilgrimage to Dick Hudson's continued through the Victorian and Edwardian periods. Then, with the coastal resorts more accessible, the practice of walking to the moors began to decline.

In Lancashire, Easter was a time to ascend Pendle Hill. It was done annually by members of the Nick o' Thung's Charity, one of those strange organisations in which comradeship, plus a touch of fantasy, made life bearable in a humdrum world. These men would escape to the wild, wearing dark suits, cloth caps, clogs and neckbands (occasionally a tie was seen). They arranged for soup to be warmed up in cauldrons for the mid-day meal. (In the West Riding they had a Greasy Chin Club, and another for hen-pecked husbands.)

Pendle Hill was the attraction for thousands, being easily accessible and cheap. A woman who climbed the Hill from Colne recalled: 'Each of us had a carrier bag with some butties and a bottle of water or milk; it depended on what we could afford. We went in clogs because they were warm. We were all singing as we walked through Barrowford to Barley, then on to the Big End of Pendle.' A Burnley man I knew walked through Newchurch to Barley, thence to Roughlee for a jug of tea in the old mill and a walk by the lake.

And in Wakes Week – as in every week-end through the year – the roads leading out of the mill towns were thronged by cycling clubs, heading for the moors and the Dales. It was a way of getting pleasure on the cheap.

The summer break was the one most keenly anticipated. Not everyone went away, but for others, the annual trip to the seaside was a blessed release from the everyday grind in a depressing environment. To a family living in the shadow of the mills, in a murky climate, breathing air that was rarely clear of smuts, there was no transition more joyous than a journey to the seaside, where the tide swept grandly on to open beaches, where the tones were light, and private enterprise had given to each resort a romantic glitter.

Whereas, in Lancashire, the annual Fair or Wakes sent waves of townsfolk to the favourite coastal resorts, the West Riding folk spread out a little further, taking in the Yorkshire coast. Their holiday weeks had quaint names: Halifax Wakes, Honley Feast, Bowling Tide (Bradford), Meltham and Ripponden Rush-bearings, Dewsbury Feast, Brighouse Rush (after the old rush-bearing ceremony) and the Spen Valley Feast (in the first week of September). The catchment area for Brighouse station would include something like 30,000 people. Of this figure, possibly no more than two or three thousand went away for a holiday – but they all went on the same day. The station was swamped.

'In the 1920s, you could go to Blackpool on the train at 5.30 p.m. and return at midnight. The cost was half a crown.' Later, the motor coaches became a premier means of transport for local holidaymakers:

> When we were young, we never went on holiday; my mum and dad couldn't afford to take us, so we got up early on the first Saturday of the holiday to watch everybody else going off. Buses extended the whole length of Bank Street, which was a long street, with a cotton mill at the end. The proprietor and his daughter stood there with clipboards, marking everybody off and telling them which coaches they were in. Every coach had a big number in the window. We stood at the bottom of the street, by a gas lamp, and the people in the buses waved at us as they passed on their way to Blackpool.

In Wakes Week, people had their annual reminder of how dirty was the normal atmosphere in town. 'Except for that week, nobody really understood what clear skies were like. Then every factory was shut down; the shops were closed. At Burnley, if you hadn't got a week's supply of bread, you'd to walk either to Brierfield in one direction, or over to Padiham in another.' When the skies cleared, people went to the summit of Crown Point at Burnley, to look round. Or from Pendle they looked for Pennine highspots like Penyghent and Ingleborough. It was said at Bolton that Wakes Week was the only time you could see the Welsh hills from the back of the town. It so happened that Leigh and Wigan were on holiday at the same time.

A Bolton friend recalled:

Everyone was in what was called a Diddle 'em Club. They put in so much money a week and drew it out just before Wakes Week. Every year – or so it seemed – someone ran off with the money belonging to one of these clubs. There would be a hue and cry for it. In the 1930s, you needed only £4 to £5 to take a family on a week's holiday. For your digs, you'd pay about £2 for the week. If you were really posh, you could have a private sitting room.

The railways were congested at Wakes Week. In Bolton, where it was necessary to go down some steps to the platforms, people despaired of getting themselves and their luggage on the same train. The railways had arrangements to issue tickets in advance, and for 2s would collect luggage and ensure its delivery. Yet half-mile long queues formed at the stations. Jimmy Fishwick, of Hellifield, who worked 'railway specials' from Hellifield into Blackpool in the days of the L & Y (Lancashire and Yorkshire railway), once arrived at Clitheroe to see so many people on the platform they were being controlled by railway police. 'When I stopped the train, there was a mad scramble to get on.' Those were the days of small compartments, with no corridor. On a train heading for Blackpool, twenty-four people might contrive to travel in a single compartment. The guard's van was always full. Up to the early 1930s there might be three thousand people leaving Clitheroe alone.

A memory of Barracks Station, Burnley, as it was before the 1914–18 war, is of porters with sleeved waistcoats standing at the edge of the platform, urging the mass of people to stand back as the train arrived. 'When the train came in, every window was packed with passengers, looking out. Kids were hanging out, clutching their buckets and spades and bunches of flags. You had to fight to get a seat.'

The celebrated Blackpool landladies would watch a host

of people staggering to their front doors. A visitor's eye view of a boarding house took in the dining room window in which was a table, holding the obligatory three bottles – brown sauce, tomato ketchup, vinegar.

In the early days, a family took much of their own food in a tin trunk, and augmented it with fresh food purchased at the holiday resort. The landlady would ask: 'Are ter goin' to board?' or 'Do I do t'lot for thee?' Most families, who had to keep their eye on expenses, merely took rooms and the landlady cooked their food for them. (Self-catering continued, to a lessening degree, until the 1930s.) A Colne family recalls:

> You took your own food and paid for what was called the 'cruet'. They charged you so much for doing your cooking. Your mother would go out in the morning and get some steak or other meat for you. The average boarding house had five families. Each had their own little cupboard for keeping things in. One would have steak, another sausage, another chops. How the landlady managed to cook for these folk when everyone seemed to get something different, I'll never know.

Ethel Gill, of Brighouse, was fifteen years old when she first saw the sea. 'It was just after the 1914–18 war; I went to Blackpool with my father and my sisters and their boyfriends. We stayed in Waterloo Road. We took some of our food, and the landlady cooked it. She provided tea, bread and butter.' A Lancashire lass who went into service at a Blackpool boarding house in 1926 – 'my mother couldn't manage to keep me' – got £1 a week and her keep. 'There were eleven bedrooms, two dining rooms and a kitchen. I'd to carry water to every bedroom every day. My mother got my £1 every week and she hadn't me to keep. So she was able to make ends meet.'

Mill lasses were determined to enjoy themselves. Some, with extravagance, would hire a horse cab at Talbot Road

Station at Blackpool and be conveyed to Yates's Wine Lodge, where port and lemon were ordered. (It made a change from Indian brandy, the term used for the medicine given by the cloth-looker at one mill if one of the weaving girls came to him, most embarrassed, because she had stomach ache at a certain time of the month!) Lancashire lasses arrived in Blackpool with 'stardust in their eyes'. Each was determined to meet a lad in romantic circumstances, which life at home could never afford. A Bolton man commented: 'Sometimes it led to better things; sometimes to worse things. Each mill girl would talk for weeks afterwards about the boy she met at Blackpool.'

A Cleckheaton family of modest means contrived to go east, to Mablethorpe:

We bought tea at Altham's every week. For every 4oz packet, we received a twopenny ticket. We saved the tickets, and by holidaytime we had enough money to take us to the East Coast. It was a difficult journey; we had to change trains five times! Just before we left home, mother packed a large tin trunk with bread, cakes, boiled tongue, ham and other food. This was all we would need to eat while on holiday. Another trunk held our clothes. By Thursday, the bread in the trunk was going mouldy, but none was wasted. Mother simply cut off the mouldy bits and we ate the rest!

The children were given tuppence a day as spending money. 'I remember they had some pierrots on the sands. Little seats were put out for children to sit on. As soon as we saw the chap with the collection box, we slid off our seats on to the sand!'

Blackpool was the place to visit. Why go elsewhere, when so much was available at the handiest stretch of the Lancashire coast? There was a sort of freedom about the place. How a Colne family, though poverty-stricken, spent a week here was told to me by one of the family:

Grandfather, who was a blacksmith, won some money at his local public house which, standing beside some waste ground, was known as 't'rat pit'. It was Wakes Week. Grandfather said to his married daughter: 'You need a holiday; I'll pay for travel and board. Take Grannie.'

Preparations had to be made. Mother bought some new black stockings, put eggs in paper, slipped the eggs into a stocking, one at a time, tying bits of string between them, so that they would not be cracked by the rigours of the journey. The train took about four hours to get to Blackpool. When it went into a siding, everybody leaned out of the window, waving at everybody else.

We stayed in Yorkshire Street, which was well known for the number of people it could sleep. Grannie, mother, my sister and me had a double bedroom. My brother went into a room with the lads of another family. It was quite a scrow [untidy mess]. Mother catered for herself; the landlady cooked the food . . . Grannie was on her best behaviour. She usually smoked a pipe. That holiday, we'd see her sitting on the bed – smoking a cigarette.

By the 1930s, a period of good and inexpensive rail services, and with private cars now quite common, those families who were not affected by industrial depression took a week's seaside holiday for granted. In 1935, Blackpool's countless landladies were wreathed in smiles: the place had been host to a total of seven million visitors between June and September.

13 Mill Town Evening

We cannot, Lord, thy purpose see, but all is well that's done by thee.

> *From the 'Deaths' column in a local newspaper*

We buried 'im wi' 'am.

> *Referring to a funeral tea featuring ham*

In the colder months of the year, dusk came early to the mill towns. The sun rose, turned in a smoky sky – and then was gone, having dipped behind the gasworks. Light drained from the stone and brick canyons of the terraces, yet when it was almost dark here, the high moors would be banded by brassy northern sunlight.

With the mill buzzers resting between shifts and with the looms silent, a mill worker, standing at the door of his house before settling down for the evening, heard few sounds beyond the clatter of railway wagons at the sidings or a tram strumming the wires as it crossed town on its shiny tracks. With only storm lanterns in use at the farms, the hills were dark, without the friendly pin-pricks of light we take for granted today. After tea, in the days before the wireless was common and when television was just a pipe-dream, chairs would be drawn up to coal fires for reflective talk, much of it about the family, continuing a tradition that surely began when early folk huddled round a fire at the mouth of a cave in the primeval world.

The Victorians had a morbid interest in death. Child mortality was high, and it was often a struggle to get through the middle years and attain a respectable old age. For one wee child at Brighouse, the news of her mother's death was shattering:

Mum died in hospital at Keighley. I didn't know she had died when I went to school that morning. Someone told me when I was on the way home. I ran every bit of the way down Smithy Carr, right up Bradford Road and into home. I just said: 'My mum hasn't died, has she?' My sister said: 'Yes, love; she has.' It was the second day of May. I was nine years old.

This girl had a little sister who had died in the January, when she was only five years old. 'She caught diphtheria. Mother gave her a lovely funeral. There were white horses and a white coach and a white coffin with blue ribbons, giving her name and when she was born and the year she died.'

Phil Smith chatted with a woman whose husband had said one day that he thought he had flu. She sent him to see the doctor, being scared of asking him to call because they could not afford to pay.

So he went up. He came home and said he had scarlet fever. I said: 'What – and me with two kids here?' He was to be away from home for six weeks. Just before the ambulance came for him I got my money out of my purse – there was just three halfpence – and went next-door to buy three cigarettes for him. While my husband was away, my little boy got pneumonia. We struggled on, with no money and no food.

The same day as my husband came home, after six weeks, the little boy died. As his dad came into the house, the little boy looked up and said: 'Daddy, daddy'. And he died. Just like that. Them were t'days, I'll tell you.

As I mentioned earlier, it was the custom for the 'dear departed' to lie in his or her coffin in the front room while his or her life was pieced together by a dozen eager gossipers. A waxy face would be scrutinised by a visitor, who would remark to the widow: 'Doesn't he look peaceful?' She would reply: 'He doesn't know he's deeard yet.' A Lancashire lad, who had just started working for a farmer, decided to drum up some extra trade while delivering milk in a mill town. When he called at one terraced house, the young lady who came to the door said: 'Do you want to see Dad?' He nodded. She took him upstairs. Dad was 'sleeping' in his coffin.

The oldest among us remember when funerals were impressive affairs, with black horses drawing large hearses, and with grief expressed in the black-edged funeral cards and special 'funeral biscuits'. As the cortège left the house, the blinds and curtains of neighbouring houses were drawn, 'out of respect'. No excessive noise was tolerated. Later, back at the house, there would be the tense sharing-out of furniture and bed-linen among the relatives, some of whom would contrive to get back gifts like half tea services which they had given to the deceased in years gone by. One family was split down the middle over the future of a long-case clock. Forty years later, they were still 'not talking' to each other!

The Lancashire writer Allen Clarke described a cab horse that was used for funerals as 'a lean, dismal horse that looked as if it had been fed on grave-wreaths and stalled in cemeteries all its life'. John Willie Lancaster, of Bradford, who was tall and thin, the epitome of the lugubrious undertaker, provided the customary black horses with long tails (some of which were false!). The rendezvous with the owner of the horses and hearse and the cabs was usually at a public house, where John Willie would buy each of the cab-drivers a gill of ale before the serious business of the day began. Sam Taylor, an undertaker at Brighouse, provided his own horses and coaches.

There seemed to be plenty of time for a funeral in those days. The horses walked slowly. Everyone in the street drew their curtains as a mark of respect. As the cortège passed, everyone stood at the side of the road. The men raised their hats. Nowadays, hearses go that fast, it's as though t'drivers think – let's get shut, right sharp!

A Colne woman whose family had little money recalls that on the death of a brother, mother hired a hearse and a single cab, which would be used for immediate relatives. 'Mother said to the others that if they wanted to attend the funeral, they must provide their own transport. So they got together, and arranged for two more cabs. Afterwards we returned to the house. Mother had cooked some meat and made some cakes. We ate them. That was that.'

Aspects of the Lancashire funeral were slow to change; in the 1970s, as one woman recalled, sometimes bodies were still placed in their coffins in private houses when, in most cases, 'chapels of rest' were in use. This girl attended the funeral of an uncle who had lived for many years in a terrace not far from Rochdale. 'Uncle was not so much lying in his coffin as propped up in it.' She detected great morbidity.

They always seemed to have the coffin open. If anybody turned up, they asked immediately to be taken to the body . . . On funeral day, there were three aunts sitting on t'settee close to where the coffin was. The parson came. There was my uncle in his coffin, and my auntie weeping over him. The coffin was closed and we went to the funeral.

One bright aspect of the day, as already mentioned, was the funeral tea, made and served by neighbours and friends. 'They had brought big teapots and extra kettles and lots of crockery to provide hot drinks for the mourners. The table was laden with good things – with ham sandwiches, meat pies, sausage rolls, teacakes, fruitcakes, all home-baked. The neighbours "waited-on" and they washed up afterwards.'

Covering the cost of a funeral had been the purpose of many of the old sick clubs that flourished. Friendly societies, such as the Rechabites, warded off the native fear of having to retire to the workhouse, or be buried 'on the parish', even after that fear had no basis because of the introduction of social security.

At Colne, one widow had an unusual floral tribute made in her husband's memory and placed on the coffin for the journey to the crematorium. The wreath was in the form of a tray holding a big pint glass, all done with brown flowers, with some white flowers at the top to represent the froth. 'After the service, we came out and saw all the flowers lying there, at the side of the path. The widow woman, noticing her special wreath, said: "That's one pint he didn't sup"!'

14 Change and Decay

I can take you to a good-looking house near here which was built from a demolished mill chimney.

A Lancashire mill director

I'd thirty-six year wi' em and finished just before mill closed down in 1953 – or was it '54? They all got redundancy pay. I got nowt.

A former mill worker, Colne

Textiles are thriving as never before. There's just one snag – it's happening mainly at t'other end of t'world.

A Yorkshire manager

Driving down the M6 on a clear December evening, I yet again saw the Lancashire conurbation represented as countless specks of orange light, as though a galaxy had fallen to earth. Strings of sodium chloride lights, many miles long, extend to infinity in a system that turns night to day. On this latest journey, I felt the modern sense of detachment from all but my immediate surroundings. For the mill towns are no longer the small, homely places that many of us recall. A strange situation has arisen whereby central areas, once so packed with mills and houses, are now open to the wind, the setting for supermarkets, garages, municipal car parks – or simply wasteland, complete with rose-bay willow-herb. At the edge of town, the new bungaloid housing growth extends remorselessly into the rural areas. The old mill town country, in Lancashire and what used to be called the West Riding, has been shredded by new roads on stilts and encircled by motorways which, in Lancashire, have the prosaic titles of M6, M61, M62 and M66.

So here I was in Lancashire, but using a multi-lane motorway, and cruising effortlessly at 70 miles an hour. Signs announcing the approaches to various towns lay only a matter of minutes apart. Should I brake now before I ran into Cheshire?

Mills that are no longer needed make excellent furniture repositories, workshops for light industries, and office suites. The first time I flew into Manchester from the east, I saw a dusting of snow on the Peak District, a gleam from those static water-tanks, the upland reservoirs, and then – stretching as far as the eye could see – what appeared to be a single, gigantic urban area, with a few mill chimneys remaining, like totems from a vanished age.

The textile industry is still large, employing some 450,000 people. But it is less conspicuous than it was. The mills are cleaner, more airy and colourful than they were in Grandfather's time. A friend claims that mill towns are tidier, cleaner, altogether nicer than they used to be. Perhaps – but they are far less interesting, I thought, as we took a short cut from the asphalt desert of the car park and through a series of supermarkets which were so stuffy you could hardly breathe, to where a modern arcade stood in all its plastic majesty. The only building worth seeing was the Victorian Town Hall.

Bales of material outside a mill in what used to be called the 'heavy woollen district' turned out to be neither wool nor cotton, but nylon, part of a consignment being used in the production of uniforms for the staff of bakeries and supermarkets. Artificial fibres have been with us since last century. Nylon, invented in the late 1930s and still very popular, washes easily, and here was being processed on water-looms – Japanese, of course – where a jet of water is used to send across what passes for a shuttle. One old mill in north-east Lancashire still reverberates to the clatter of Lancashire looms. It is weaving not cotton or flannelette – but parachute material!

Past and present are part of a continuous process. A weaving firm owned by a company with a household name still rents their accommodation from a shed company founded at the start of the century. Five little firms operated here until the present company took over sixty years ago. Until quite recent times, the company had 520 Lancashire looms and 145 operatives; then the mill was re-equipped with eighty-five rapid-action shuttleless looms, operated on a shift system – by forty-four people. The loss of one hundred jobs was a shame for future job prospects, but did not unduly worry those who had been displaced by more efficient machines. 'They worked it out that th'average age of workers was fifty-six. So they had a good redundancy scheme. Wife and I haven't clamm'd [starved] since I left.'

The old Lancashire looms had produced about 18.5 million metres of cloth a year. Roughly the same output was now being achieved by a few modern looms. The manager of this company quoted figures to show that in 1926, from the Yorkshire/Lancashire border at Earby as far as Manchester, there were about 780,000 looms. 'Now I reckon there'll be 22,000. I don't think I'll be far out.' One of the last of the hand-twisters demonstrated, with nimble fingers, what had to be performed by one of the old machines. This one, a Barber Coleman knotting machine, kept as a curiosity, was made in America in 1906.

The tackler, who was the butt of many a joke, is now the textile technician, with an office and a cordless telephone. The twister I met had a fund of good stories about tacklers, including one about the jape involving tying a tackler's pot (mug) to a vice on the bench. When the tackler collected the pot, either he left the handle attached to the vice, or 'it'd smash t'pot altogether'. No one seems to bother much about japes today.

The textile story has been one of change and decay. 'The seeds of destruction came almost at its conception. After all, when we are born we are on the way to dying,' said a former manager. Here was no trace of morbidity, just a recognition that change is in the nature of things. He listed some of the factors in the decline – outdated machines, more expensive labour, two world wars and the loss of overseas markets; and the importation of cheaper foreign cloth and of outstanding semi-automatic looms from France, Switzerland and Italy. In the early 1960s, when the government, with cash incentives, made it attractive for private companies to disband, many firms who had full order books closed down. There had been damaging fluctuations in the value of the pound, favouring our overseas competitors. 'Textiles,' said this former manager, speaking generally, 'have moved into the hands of large public companies.'

He summarised the present situation: 'The textile industry has been modernised and there is a certain amount of fighting back.' Fighting back? 'Yes,' he responded. 'We have bought cotton cloth from China at 15 per cent cheaper than we could make it. But when we had finished throwing away from 12 to 15 per cent of the cloth that didn't meet our standards, I suddenly realised I was very competitive. I do at least know that what comes off my machines is first-quality cloth.' Wool, a premier fibre, is less important than it was. 'People wear clothing now, not necessarily to keep warm, but for fashion. Men want to look smart and women want to look pretty. Women discard clothes with alacrity. I think that my daughter has thrown more clothes away this week than my wife had in her entire wardrobe when she was twenty-four years old.' Traditionally, the overcoat was either blue or grey. Overcoats are still being made, but at nowhere near the old level of production, and they are being turned out in various colours, to suit the fancy of modern customers.

I walked through a weaving shed that had those generous Edwardian proportions, attractive 'northern lights' and a roof supported by cast-iron pillars carrying a little ornamentation. Eighty modern looms, most of them operating without the immediate attention of a technician – he was hardly a weaver, in the old sense – were running without excessive noise.

With me was a mill worker of over forty years' experience. He reminded me of the times when a tackler shouldered a warp and carried it down an alley, between clattering looms and swishing leather belts, any one of which could inflict injury. 'Now we are talking about 20,000 metres on a weaver's beam. And that is sufficient for only about four weeks. Each loom produces over 1000 metres of cloth a day on three shifts. Weaving has certainly taken off, compared with the old days.' The modern loom stops instantly if a warp or weft breaks.

T'owd Lancashire loom just clattered on. They did start 'pinning' it later on, but if they weren't pinned it wouldn't make any difference if the weft broke or an end came down in the warp. It would just run on, with that end down, till it got reight fast-up. Weaver had to go to t'tackler and say: 'Eh – it's weavin' baht weft again.' Many a time there'd be yards of warp gone through and nowt in it!

Where there's muck, there's money. 'When the old shop finished, and we smashed a lot o' looms up for scrap, in about 1976, cast iron was bringing about £35 or £40 a ton. So there was quite a lot o' money made out of th'Lancashire loom job when they were no longer needed.'

I walked across the town, passing a car park where once a mill had stood. Also in view was a furniture repository that had been adapted from a chapel, and a supermarket that had succeeded a range of Co-op shops. A pensioner, who had once worked in th'mill, was waiting for a bus after a shopping excursion. He said of his native mill town, now so radically different from the one in which he had grown up: 'They've mucked t'place up, but I still like it. I couldn't fall out wi' it, however much I tried. Aye, if I won t'pools, I wouldn't fancy living anywhere else. I'd stay on mi own ground.'

We looked down a street of terraced housing and between two remaining chimneys to where Pendle Hill stood, with weather-seamed slopes and a bonnet of cloud. 'If that owd hill could talk,' said the old man, 'I reckon he'd have some reight good tales to tell . . .'

Appendix: The Textile Heritage

Styal Country Park, one of the possessions of the National Trust, lies in a part of Cheshire that has been shredded by motorways and is within an easy distance of Manchester Airport. My first visit was prompted by a colourful brochure inviting me to explore the past.

The copywriter's enthusiasm for his subject was infectious: 'Whoosh. Whoosh. The giant waterwheel turns and turns relentlessly. Fifty tons of iron, twenty-four feet high, looming in the gloom. Built to power four floors of machinery inside the Mill. Row upon row of looms, weaving away, producing an incessant deafening clatter . . .'

I could not reconcile such industry with what I knew of Cheshire and, indeed, this mill proved to be Georgian in style and in a thoroughly rural setting, distinguished by greensward, fine trees and an unpolluted River Bollin. I chose first to explore the other attractions of this area. It was an easy walk from Mill to Apprentice House, where pauper children were quartered, sleeping two to a bed, which was good by nineteenth-century standards. Along Apprentice Lane lay Chapels, School, Oak Farm and Cottages. The apprentices had once occupied a good part of Sunday in walking two miles to attend church in Wilmslow.

Then I returned to the Mill, still finding it hard to believe that such a fine building in this idyllic spot had been concerned with something as sordid as work. Pictures and captions introduced me to the Gregs of Styal; they had been here for generations, and they adapted to change without sacrificing the quality of the buildings or their setting. Here was arranged, graphically, using machines still capable of work, the long and complex story of textiles. After watching a woman at a spinning wheel and another operating one of Mr Kay's looms – each dressed in old-fashioned attire – I visited a floor where stood the cast-iron machines I had seen in many a commercial mill, and especially the Lancashire loom, the products of which were once despatched to all parts of the world.

Something of the spirit of the old mill town life endures in many another working museum, and in undeveloped parts of Lancashire and Yorkshire. The curators of museums long since broke away from the rigid idea of arranging objects neatly in rows under glass: the working museum is commonplace and the comparatively new pursuit of industrial archaeology, once thought of as a crankish occupation, is now respectable.

Preservation groups, consisting of cheerful volunteers with spanners and oily rags, restore mill engines, Lancashire looms, even railways, and they operate them for our wonderment and delight. So in our north country travels we may still have a whiff of acrid smoke (very evocative stuff) or have the dank smell of a humid weaving shed in our nostrils; we may even now listen to the whirr and clatter of old machinery operated by leathern belting that smacks itself and creates a furious draught in lofty galleries.

A walk along the canal bank in any industrial town offers views of old mills and associated buildings. Burnley and Leeds are just two which promote such walks as tourist features. The forest of mill chimneys has been greatly pruned of late, but it is still possible to stand near the base of a chimney and, risking neckache, look up at an impressive structure of dressed stone or Accrington brick.

My favourite little mill towns, when I wish to wander over stone setts and between terrace houses, are Nelson and Colne. The visitor may see a mill chimney looming at the end of the street and, of course, there will be a corner shop. Such an area is full of mill-town characters, both young and old.

The following list of textile attractions is not exhaustive, being based on personal experience. Details of opening times were correct at the time of writing. A telephone call to the selected place for confirmation is recommended in advance of a visit by those who must travel long distances. With the easy mobility of the modern car, it is possible to fit in three or four attractions in a day.

BANCROFT MILL ENGINE
Gillians Lane, off Colne Road, Barnoldswick, Lancashire. Telephone inquiries to David Normanshire (0282) 813751.

The engine is a 600 bhp cross compound Corliss valve condensing steam, with a speed of 68 rpm, and a flywheel with a diameter of 16 feet and a weight of 30 tons. It was built by William Roberts & Sons, at Phoenix Foundry, Nelson, and drove 1,250 looms.

The Bancroft Engine Trust was formed in 1980 to preserve what had become the last working steam mill engine in the small town of Barnoldswick, which in its industrial heyday had 13 mills. The engine house, with adjacent building for the boilers, and a brick chimney are all that remain of the mill.

Bancroft Mill was a latecomer, being built as recently as 1920 by James Nutter. The engine has two cylinders, and he named the high pressure cylinder after himself and gave his wife's name, Mary Jane, to the low pressure cylinder. A note in the leaflet of the Bancroft Mill Engine Trust states: 'It is not known whether the intended impression was that they were both working together or it was his idea of their relative status.'

'Steaming days', in conjunction with cotton weaving displays, take place at prescribed times between March and October. Steam from the boiler at 160 lb per square inch is first expanded in the high pressure cylinder, and 'James' turns the flywheel over. There being still some energy in the steam, it is passed across to the low pressure cylinder, and 'Mary Jane', by re-using the steam, gives the wheel a further turn.

The exhausted steam is then piped to the condenser in the basement to be turned back into re-usable water. A mill dam no longer exists. The Lancashire boiler, housed in a building adjacent to the engine house, was one of the largest of its type to be built.

The location of the Bancroft engine is indicated by a signpost in Barnoldswick. 'Steaming days' are advertised locally, or a telephone call to David Normanshire will yield information about dates when the engine will next be in use. The opening times are from 1 p.m. to 5 p.m. A charge is made for admission. Refreshments are available.

BOLTON STEAM MUSEUM

Atlas No. 3 Mill, Chorley Old Road, Bolton. For details, ring Jim Jones at (0204) 74557 or Tim Hanson at Rochdale (0706) 58528.

The museum, a converted engine house, now owned by the Northern Mill Engine Society, is just over a mile north-west of the town centre. In a spacious setting, six steam engines, some of which are more than a century old, are displayed. In the assembly are an 1840 twin beam engine, an 1860 'A-frame' vertical, a 1902 horizontal tandem and an 1893 'non-dead-centre' engine, built in Bolton.

Each engine was fully restored and re-built. Steam days are organised.

BRADFORD INDUSTRIAL MUSEUM
Moorside Mills, Moorside Broad, Bradford, BD2 3HP. Tel:
(0274) 631756.

The museum lies to the north-east of the city centre and
is signposted from the Ring Road and Harrogate Road.

In this former spinning mill are steam engines, plus the
machines which once converted raw wool into worsted
cloth. Moorside House, home of the mill-owner and his
family, has been restored and furnished as they would
have known it. The museum has a transport gallery and
Bradford's last tram. Shop and café.

Open Tuesday–Sunday and Bank Holiday Mondays, 10
a.m. to 5 p.m. Admission free.

CALDERDALE INDUSTRIAL MUSEUM
Square Road, Halifax. Tel: (0422) 358087.

This museum is adjacent to Halifax's Piece Hall, which
has been described as one of Europe's most outstanding
eighteenth-century buildings. The Piece Hall was constructed as a market for homespun cloth in the heyday of
the domestic wool industry.

The Industrial Museum has steam engines, working
looms (and even toffee wrapping machines, Halifax being
the home of Mackintosh's). Visitors are invited to 'crawl
through a coal and clay mine and wander the streets of
the Halifax of 1850'.

The premises are open from Tuesday to Saturday, 10
a.m. to 5 p.m., and on Sunday from 2 p.m. to 5 p.m.
Although normally closed on Monday, an exception is
made for Bank Holidays.

A complementary attraction at Halifax is Shibden Hall,
a half-timbered house of the early fifteenth century, in the
grounds of which is a folk museum arranged to represent
a village in the early nineteenth century.

ELLENROAD ENGINE HOUSE
Milnrow, Rochdale. No telephone. The Rochdale Tourist Information Office may be contacted on (0706) 356592.

Ellenroad engine house stands next to Junction 21 (the Milnrow exit) on the M62. Turn under the motorway as if you are travelling to Shaw and take the first turn to the right.

This enterprise, a coal-fired boiler house and working steam engine, is open to the public at weekends, and guided tours are arranged. The project is run by the Ellenroad Mill Trust, on which are represented the owners of the steam engine, Messrs Coates, Rochdale Corporation and the Friends of Ellenroad. The project manager is Stanley Graham.

Visitors on 'steaming' days see an engine of awesome power – the largest complete example of a steam engine left in Britain – generating up to 3,000 hp. The flywheel, which is 28 feet in diameter, weighs 85 tons. It has been calculated that the weight is equal to nine double-decker buses. The engine is used in conjunction with one of the five original Lancashire boilers and with a coal-stoker that served the former Oldham Royal Infirmary.

HELMSHORE TEXTILE MUSEUMS
Holcombe Road, Helmshore, Rossendale, Lancashire, BB4 4NP. Tel: (0706) 226459. The Textile Museums are run by Lancashire County Council.

Helmshore lies on the B6235, one mile south of Haslingden. The eighteenth-century fulling mill, with a splendid nineteenth-century waterwheel, has long been established as a working museum. A visitor is provided with demonstrations of Hargreaves' Spinning Jenny, Arkwright's Water Frame and Spinning Mules. The mill has an attractive setting with a riverside walk and picnic area. There is an admission charge, and guided tours by arrangement.

Opening hours: Easter to June 30 and October, Monday to Friday 2 p.m. to 5 p.m. July to September 30, Monday to Friday, 12 noon to 5 p.m., Saturday 2 p.m. to 5 p.m. Easter to October 31, Sunday, 11 a.m. to 5 p.m. November to Easter, Sunday, 2 p.m. to 5 p.m. Open Bank Holiday weekends except Christmas Day, Boxing Day and New Year's Day.

Rossendale Museum, in Whitaker Park, Rawtenstall, is a former mill-owner's mansion.

LEEDS CLOTH TRAIL
For more details contact Leeds City Tourism at Tel: (0532) 463223.

The first section of the Cloth Trail is of most interest to industrial archaeologists. It follows the wool from its arrival at the Leeds and Liverpool Docks at Granary Wharf up to Booth's Yard at Pudsey, where it was spun and woven, and on to Armley Mills, where it was fulled.

Armley Mills were once the world's largest woollen mills, built to card the weaver's wool ready for spinning and to 'full' the woven cloth, which was beaten with water-powered hammers as it lay wet in a deep trough.

LEWIS TEXTILE MUSEUM

At Blackburn. The Museum, which is adjacent to the Museum and Art Gallery, features cotton processing.

PENDLE HERITAGE CENTRE
Park Hill, Barrowford, Nelson. Tel: (0282) 695366.

A historic house which is just off the A682 at the edge of Barrowford Park. This centre is the regional base for heritage education and interpretation. Exhibitions. Audio-visual presentation and shop. Open for Exhibitions: Easter to November, 2 p.m. to 4 p.m.

PROVIDENCE MILLS
Syke Lane, Earlsheaton, Dewsbury, West Yorkshire. Tel: (0924) 465191.

The mill has a showroom, with fabric, wall coverings and furniture. Steam days are held when the mill engine 'Sara' is the star. She is a unique 300 hp horizontal tandem, compound, engine.

QUARRY BANK MILL
In Styal Country Park, Cheshire, just north of Wilmslow off the B5166, M56 Junction 5.

As already stated, this property is owned by the National Trust and Styal is splendidly managed by the Trust's tenants, Quarry Bank Mill Trust, Ltd. (See the National Trust guide book for details of opening times or telephone Wilmslow (0625) 527468). Charges for admission except for National Trust members who produce membership cards.

The showpiece of this all-the-year-round attraction is a Georgian cotton mill, on four floors, formerly owned by the Greg family who were pioneers of the factory system. The mill, and its 24-foot diameter waterwheel, has been restored as a working museum of the cotton industry.

Visitors are treated to demonstrations of spinning and weaving, including examples of the improved technology leading to the Industrial Revolution. Also *in situ*, and working, are the impressive products of North Country foundries, including spinning frames and Lancashire looms, in full working order. The workers are in period dress. One gallery is decked with illustrations of the world of the former owners and their workers. The mill has a shop and catering facilities.

For many, the abiding memories are of the newly restored Apprentice House, where 100 young paupers were quartered; they received a penny ha'penny a day and attended school at night. This house is furnished according to its period and the use to which it was put. In a crock in the doctor's room are live leeches, used for 'letting' blood. The adjacent garden is maintained as it would have been 150 years ago.

QUEEN STREET MILL MUSEUM
Harle Syke, Burnley. Tel: (0282) 412555.

The mill is located on the right off Briercliffe Road, some ten minutes from the centre of Burnley. Admission charge.

I have a special regard for Queen Street Mill. Although it caters for visitors, it is not touristy. Here is the only surviving steam-powered cotton mill in Britain. It dates from 1894, which was the heyday of milldom, when Burnley was acknowledged to be the weaving centre of the world.

Queen Street is still a working mill, with large rooms, a lofty brick chimney, a dam (visited by anglers!) and the steam engine (an immaculate creature named 'Peace'). A visitor who sees rows of chattering Lancashire looms has a real insight into Victorian factory life.

The future of Queen Street has been in doubt, but now seems assured and refurbishment is taking place. The steam engine, and attendant machines, operate on Wednesday, Thursday and Friday, between 10.30 a.m. and 3.30 p.m. Confirmation is possible by using the telephone number above. For other local attractions of an industrial nature, ring the Burnley Tourist Information Office on (0282) 30055.

WEAVERS' TRIANGLE VISITOR CENTRE
85a Manchester Road, Burnley. Tel: (0282) 30055.

The centre is situated at the top of Manchester Road, some five minutes from the centre of Burnley. A walker on the towpath of the Leeds and Liverpool canal sees one of England's best-preserved industrial landscapes, with weaving sheds, spinning mills, warehouses, foundries where steam engines and looms were made, domestic buildings and a school.

The Weavers' Triangle is accessible all the year round. The Visitor Centre, formerly the wharfmaster's house and canal toll office in Manchester Road, has a basement room which has been arranged to represent a weaver's dwelling. The centre is open on Tuesday, Wednesday, Saturday and Sunday, from 2 p.m. to 4 p.m. Admission is free. Hot drinks are available.

WORTH VALLEY RAILWAY
Haworth Station, Keighley, West Yorkshire. Tel: (0535) 643629.

The railway was a vital part of Victorian industrial life, shifting goods and people speedily and economically. The Keighley and Worth Valley Railway, a five-mile branch, built by a company formed mainly of local mill-owners, was opened in 1867.

The line was closed in 1961, but is now owned by a preservation society which restored the track, stations and equipment and now provides a steam train service every weekend, and daily during the summer. Special 'steam' occasions are organised.

The Worth Valley line has often been used by film companies. Sequences for the most recent film version of that popular Victorian story, *The Railway Children*, were shot hereabouts.

YORKSHIRE MINING MUSEUM
Caphouse Colliery, New Road, Overton, Wakefield. Tel: (0924) 848806.

The museum is situated beside the A642 between Wakefield and Huddersfield. Easy access is possible from both the M1 and M62.

Coal powered the Industrial Revolution. Coal fires kept the urban populace warm (and clouded the air with acrid smoke). Caphouse Colliery, like many another, has a rural setting. Here a visitor might ride the cage to an area that is 450 feet underground. Experienced miners guide visitors through authentic workings.

The museum and Visitor Centre are open every day throughout the year (except December 25, 26 and January 1) from 10 a.m. to 5 p.m.

Index